LAST LETTERS
FROM THE LIVING
DEAD MAN

LAST LETTERS FROM THE LIVING DEAD MAN

by

ELSA BARKER

Last Letters from the Living Dead Man

White Crow Books is an imprint of
White Crow Productions Ltd
PO Box 1013
Guildford
GU1 9EJ

www.whitecrowbooks.com

Text design and eBook production by Essential Works
www.essentialworks.co.uk

ISBN 978-1-907355-87-5
eBook ISBN 978-1-907355-88-2

Religion & Spirituality

Distributed in the UK by
Lightning Source Ltd.
Chapter House
Pitfield
Kiln Farm
Milton Keynes MK11 3LW

Distributed in the USA by
Lightning Source Inc.
246 Heil Quaker Boulevard
LaVergne
Tennessee 37086

Contents

Introduction

THIS BOOK, THE third and last of the *Living Dead Man* series, was written between February 1917, and February 1918. Then I lost the ability— or perhaps I should say the inclination to do automatic writing. As this third manuscript was shorter than the other two, I had supposed it to be a fragment which would probably never be finished; and it was not until my publisher urged me to issue it *as* a fragment that I read it all over for the first time and discovered that it was really a complete thing, an organic whole.

"Perhaps," I told myself, surprised and still half-incredulous, "there *is* a divinity that shapes our ends." For had the book been published when it was written, it would have seemed premature; now the greater part of it is timely as yesterday's editorials. For the benefit of those who have not read the earlier books of the series, *Letters From a Living Dead Man*, 1914, and *War Letters From the Living Dead Man*, 1915, I will quote from the introductions of those books. In the first Introduction I said:

"One night last year in Paris I was strongly impelled to take up a pencil and write, though what I was to write about I had no idea. Yielding to the impulse, my hand was seized as if from the outside, and a remarkable message of a personal nature came, followed by the signature 'X.'

"The purport of the message was clear, but the signature puzzled me. "The following day I showed this writing to a friend, asking her if she had any idea who 'X' was. "Why," she replied, "don't you know that that is what we always call Mr.—?" I did not know. Now Mr.— was six thousand miles from Paris, and, as we supposed, in the land of the living. But a day or two later a letter came to me from America, stating that Mr.— had died in the western part of the United States, a few days before I received in Paris the automatic message signed "X." So far as I know, I was the first person in Europe to be informed of his death, and I immediately called on my friend to tell her that 'X' had passed out. She did not seem surprised, and told me that she had felt certain of it some days before, when I had shown her the 'X' letter, though she had not said so at the time. "Naturally I was impressed by this extraordinary incident....

"But to the whole subject of communication between the two worlds I felt an unusual degree of indifference. Spiritualism had always left me quite cold, and I had not even read the ordinary standard works on the subject. Several letters signed 'X' were automatically written during the next few weeks; but, instead of becoming enthusiastic, I developed a strong disinclination for this manner of writing, and was only persuaded to continue it through the arguments of my friend that if 'X' really wished to communicate with the world, I was highly privileged in being able to help him. Gradually, as I conquered my strong prejudice against automatic writing, I became interested in the things which 'X' told me about the life beyond the grave....

"When it was first suggested that these letters should be published with an introduction by me, I did not take very enthusiastically to the idea. Being the author of several books, more or less well known, I had my little vanity as to the stability of my literary reputation. I did not wish to be known as eccentric, a 'freak.' But I consented to write an introduction stating that the letters were automatically written in my presence, which would have been the truth, though not all the truth. This satisfied my friend; but as time went on, it did not satisfy me. It seemed not quite sincere. I argued the matter out with myself. The letters were probably two-thirds written before this question was finally settled; and I decided that if I published the letters at all, I should publish them with a frank introduction, stating the exact circumstances of their reception by me. The interest aroused by *Letters From a Living Dead Man*, which had been published simultaneously in London and New York, astonished me. Requests for translation rights began to come in, and I was flooded with letters from all parts of the world. I answered as many as I could, but to answer all was quite impossible.

Now I will quote again, briefly, from the Introduction to the second volume, *War Letters From the Living Dead Man*, 1915:

"In that first book of 'X' I did not state who the writer was, not feeling at liberty to do so without the consent of his family; but in the summer of 1914, while I was still living in Europe, a long interview with Mr. Bruce Hatch appeared in the *New York Sunday World*, in which he expressed the conviction that the *Letters* were genuine communications from his father, the late Judge David P. Hatch, of Los Angeles, California. "After the *Letters* were finished in 1913, during a period of about two years I was conscious of the presence of 'X' only on two or three occasions, when he wrote some brief advice in regard to my personal affairs.

On the fourth of February 1915, in New York, I was suddenly made aware one day that 'X' stood in the room and wished to write; but as always before, with one or two exceptions, I had not the remotest idea of what he was going to say. He wrote as follows: "When I come back and tell you the story of this war, as seen from the other side, you will know more than all the Chancelleries of the nations." Then I went on to describe the process of my automatic writing, adding:

"No person who had had even a minute fraction of my occult experience could be more coldly critical of that experience than I am. I freely welcome every logical argument against the belief that these letters are what they purport to be; but placing those arguments in opposition to the evidence which I have of the genuineness of them, the affirmations outweigh the denials, and I accept them. This evidence is too complex and much of it too personal to be even outlined here."

The second volume, which dealt with the war from the hidden side of things, and predicted the victory of the Allies, aroused even more interest than the first one. The flood of letters continued. In 1916, at the kind insistence of Joyce Kilmer, I published another and different little book of automatic writings, *Songs of a Vagrom Angel*, the angel being the Beautiful Being described by 'X' in the *Living Dead Man* books. The *Songs* were charmingly received by the critics. The whole book, with the exception of three of the songs, had been "written down" in twenty-two hours. In the summer of 1916 I went to California, and it was there, in February 1917, that the writing of this third book began. But I was growing more and more restive at the swamping of my literary career by automatic writings, and my mountainous correspondence left me less and less time for original work. Finally, in February 1918, the "inner conflict" culminated in a complete cessation of automatic writing.

The artist in me had become exasperated. If the reader will permit the exaggeration of the simile, I felt as a man might feel who was caught between the jaws of a lion that was carrying him away into a trackless jungle. Before March 1914, I had been known as a poet and a novelist; since 1914 my name had become known in more countries than I have counted as a "psychic," a medium of communication between the visible and the invisible worlds. I was not sorry that I had published the books, because so many people had written me that I had saved them from despair and even suicide; but I shrank from the publicity they brought me. I have been nearly devoured by these books and the readers of these books. I felt, in February 1918, that I had a right to say that the incident was closed.

But that did not mean a cessation of correspondence. Suffering souls to whose letters the limitations of time and uncertain health (for I had not been well since 1915) made it impossible to respond by return of post, would write again reproaching me with indifference to their sufferings. The situation had become inconceivable. And if I went out somewhere for an hour or two of social "rest," I was surrounded by people who wanted me to talk to them about the 'X' books, about their own dead friends, and the possibilities of communication.

I was torn by pity for those who were suffering, and after years of war nearly everyone was suffering; but I wanted to be at the front with the Red Cross, and my health would not permit me to go. I could help various war committees, but I could not go to my tortured and beloved France—to be perhaps an added burden, should I break down altogether. The only escape from this conflict was in abstruse studies, studies where pure mind can work. So I seriously took up Analytical Psychology, in which I had been mildly interested since 1915. Some fourteen hours a day for a year I studied, some of the time with a teacher, some of the time alone. I burrowed under the theories of the Three Great Schools, and synthesized them, after my fashion. I had rather an active mind to experiment upon—my own. The "resistances," so-called, had been broken down by the teacher.

One of the things which appealed most to my reason was Jung's insistence upon the psychological (and therefore practical) value of the irrational. He says:

"There is no human foresight nor philosophy which can enable us to give our lives a prescribed direction, except for quite a short distance. Destiny lies before us, perplexing us, and teeming with possibilities, and yet only one of these many possibilities is our own particular right way. Much can certainly be attained by will power. But our will is a function that is directed by our powers of reflection. Has it ever been proved, or can it ever be proved, that life and destiny harmonize with our human reason, that is, that they are exclusively rational? On the contrary, we have ground for supposing that they are also irrational, that is to say, that in the last resort they too are based in regions beyond the human reason. The irrationality of the great process is shown by its so-called *accidentalness*. The rich store of life both is, and is not, determined by law; it is at the same time rational and irrational. Therefore, the reason and the will founded upon it are only valid for a short distance. The further we extend this rationally chosen direction, the surer we may be that we are thereby excluding the irrational possibilities of life, which have, however, just as good a right to be lived. Aye, we may injure ourselves, since we cut off the wealth of accidental eventualities by a too rigid and conscious direction. The present fearful catastrophic world-war has tremendously upset the most optimistic upholder of rationalism and culture."

Now my rationally chosen "line of life" had been that of writing books of poetry, fiction and essays. But "accidentalness" cut in, and I wrote automatically and published what I had written. That destiny, that second line of life, may also have been, for all we can prove to the contrary, based "in regions beyond the human reason."

I should not like to say that having led the way, in the spring of 1914, for writers of dignified reputation to publish their automatic writings might have been casually directed by the coming great need of the world for spiritual consolation during the most awful holocaust in history. That would be pressing irrationality too far. But that second line of life, as Jung would call it, came to its inevitable end with the last of this manuscript in February 1918. The cause of that was also seemingly accidental. But as this Introduction is only an introduction, it is impossible to follow the course of all the drops of water in the broad river that has flowed under my mental bridges during the last fourteen months.

My present line of life (and through the analysis of my dreams I have means of knowing what it is) points to the resumption of my original literary work, poetry, fiction and essays, and to the exclusion, so far as possible, of everything that would deflect me from that course. "Accidents" will cut in from time to time, change of place and therefore change of outlook, studies of all sorts, and legitimate demands by that society of which I form a part; but I have done enough automatic writing. Others will do it, if it must be done; and probably it must—because it is an outlet which it might be unsafe to stop up in the present state of the race consciousness. Of course if I should feel strongly impelled to do automatic writing, I should do it, trusting to that destiny which is another name for causes beyond our comprehension; but it was the strength of my "inner protest" that made me realize that I had gone far enough along that line.

As in the forewords to the former books, I state the psychological situation of the moment, saying, "so and so happened." The reader, as before, will interpret in his own way. This introduction indicates my point of view in the month of April 1919. Before the month of May 2019, I shall have solved the problem of survival, or demonstrated (without knowing it) that it is insoluble. The more we know about all these things, the less likely we are to assume that we have the sum of all knowledge. We are like children, groping among psychological lights and shadows.

My own belief in immortality seems ineradicable. I did not know that until it was tested out. But we must always remember that our personal belief is not absolute evidence of the truth of what we believe—at least until we shall have examined all the psychological roots of the belief, and in the present state of our knowledge that is well nigh impossible. Our rational belief, if we have formed one for ourselves and have not merely accepted uncritically the beliefs of our predecessors and associates, is merely our individual synthesis. But we must not give an exaggerated value even to our own hard-won synthesis. That also is a moving, an ever changing thing. Otherwise we should not grow. When a man becomes fixed he begins to disintegrate.

In the first book of this series I stated in fact that I had never been interested in spiritualism. Consciously, I never had. Now, Dr. Alfred Adler, the head of what we may call the Ego School of analysis, says: "Often the negation is the assertion of an old interest that has become conscious." Yes. My father was deeply interested in spiritualism, and I was born in an old house where ghosts were supposed to walk. My mother was afraid of the subject. My father died when I was thirteen. I was always a little afraid of my father. The first time I met Judge Hatch I told him that perhaps he had been my father in a "former incarnation." He smiled, and said, "Maybe." No microscopist had ever a greater interest in facts than I have. My scientific friends say, "A scientist was lost in you." Other friends say, "You are a great psychic." So there I found myself. In studying with the scientific half the phenomena of the psychic half, I am able to unify them.

The *authority* of the Church has been knocked from under us. We are adrift, we thinking humans of the early twentieth century, upon a sea of mind, storm-tossed by winds of feeling. We were just beginning to believe in universal brotherhood—when universal war broke out. Our steersman seemed to have been washed overboard. Everybody wants to take the helm, distrusting his neighbor's judgment. Is it any wonder that bewildered souls by thousands turned to automatic writing, seeking for guidance, for something *authoritative?* In childhood our parents guided us. Later the Church guided us—or tried to. Then science guided us—a little too far. And in the reaction we turned inward, to find (sometimes) the unconscious more troubled than the conscious. But in the *Letters* which follow there is no despair, only light and courage and hope.

There seem to be two main streams in us, the mental and the instinctive. Bergson says, in his *Creative Evolution*, "There are things which intelligence alone is able to seek, but which, by itself, it will never find. These things instinct alone could find; but it will never seek them." It was inevitable that modern psychology, with its constructive curiosity, should turn its attention to the religious beliefs of the past and present. There was no other way of understanding what really goes on in the minds of people. Some of these old beliefs proved, on examination, to be scientifically tenable. For instance, the Theosophists (who got the idea from the Hindus) tell us there are two streams of information, the elemental and the human. Dr. C. J. Jung, the head of the Swiss School of Analytical Psychology, divides the stream of "energy" into two currents, one going forward and one going backward. And this duality of will Bleuler calls "ambitendency." The difference is chiefly a difference of phraseology and associations.

"Always a pull of the opposites," I quote from the *Letters* which follow. The present psychic wave which is sweeping over the world is accompanied by modern analytical psychology. Truth may lie in the synthesis.

Between the credulity of those who believe everything purporting to come from the other side of the veil, who accept every suggestion from anybody claiming to be "psychic" who half-closes the eyes and says dreamily, "You will do so and so"—between this thirst for delusion and the materialists' denial that there is anything but matter and the functions of *matter*, there is also a middle ground.

The great pioneer of analytical psychology himself said, in a recent little volume on *War and Death*, translated by Dr. A. A. Brill: "In the unconscious every one of us is convinced of his own immortality." Suppose the unconscious should be right? And, by the way, between the statement of Christian Scientists, "All is love," and the statement of the parent school of psychoanalysis, "All is libido," there is striking similarity. Jung would say, "All is energy." Judge Hatch wrote, in a little book published in 1905, "We postulate immortal Units of Force, each having the power to generate a constant but limited amount of energy, and no two alike in quantity. Upon this force generation in the unit, necessitated by law, do we base life. Life results from the inter-dealing and inter-playing of these units among themselves eternally, sometimes potential, again kinetic, each limited in the amount of force generated, but unlimited in variety of motion, manifestation or specialization."

Truth may indeed be one, though the roads to it are many. Fechner's assertion, that the dead live in us and so influence us, does not require much stretching to fit the hypothesis that the entire past of the human race is contained in the deeper levels of the unconscious. If we go deep enough in analysis that hypothesis is illustrated by strange phenomena. It is unwise, at the present time more than any other, even to try to take away man's belief in immortality. The world is too sad, too near the ragged edge where personal uncertainty drifts into social irresponsibility. The psychic wave that is sweeping over the world, though it is being carried to excess, as all over-compensations are, answers nevertheless to a tremendous need. Credulity is the other end of doubt.

Dr. Smith Ely Jelliffe, in the Introduction to his translation of Silberer's *Problems of Mysticism and Its Symbolism*, says:

"Much of the strange and *outré*, as well as the commonplace, in human activity conceal energy transformations of inestimable value in the work of sublimation. The race would go mad without it. It sometimes does even with it, a sign that sublimation is still imperfect and that the race is far from being spiritually well. A comprehension of the principles here involved would further the spread of sympathy for all forms of thinking and tend to further spiritual health in such mutual comprehension of the needs of others and of the forms taken by sublimation processes."

William James defended the Christian Scientists. And Jung himself says, in one of his famous letters to Dr. Loy, "Every method is good if it serves its purpose, including Christian Science, Mental Healing, etc." During the last five years man has had such varied reasons for fearing objective things that he has come to fear the subjective, perhaps even more than during the Middle Ages. Dr. H. W. Frink says, in his masterly book on *Morbid Fears and Compulsions*: "The biological function or purpose of fear is protective or preservative. Every one of us alive today owes his existence to the fact that his human and pre-human ancestors were afraid." Nearly everyone is afraid of something. Sublime Jeanne d'Arc was terribly afraid of the fire. (Perhaps she had been badly burned in infancy, and the unconscious memory twisted and turned in the deeps of her pure soul. Perhaps, and perhaps, for we shall never know.)

When we really know what fear is, we shall have solve the mystery of "the one and the many" that disturbed the cerebration of our ancestors. Fear may be a momentary surging up of the ego's consciousness of its own helpless littleness before the immensity of the unknown and unknowable non-ego. The reckless courage of the soldier may be an over-compensation, a triumphant sublimation—sometimes followed by reaction, secret or unconcealable, depending on the intensity. For, as Silberer says, "The conflicts do not indeed lie in the external world, but in our *emotional disposition towards it*; if we change this disposition by an inner development, the external world has a different value."

Man is indeed his own cosmos, the microcosm of the macrocosm, to a degree incomprehensible to one who has not intelligently studied (and in himself) the phenomena of "projection," and compensation including sublimation. The great mystics of all ages, through introversion, having discovered this and reduced it to a science, after their fashion, great modern scientists like Jung and Silberer have found their systems worthy of profound study. Writing of mysticism, Professor Dwelshauvers of Brussels says:

"The effects of mystic union are logical and coherent; a second quality of the acts of the order of grace is the positive character of the contribution, the increase which they bring to the psychic life of those who benefit by them. The idea of God, the divine presence, or any other form of inspiration, is no more strange to the mind of the religious man than is for the *savant* the sudden conception of a solution long sought for, or for the artist the vision of the work which he meditates and of which he pursues the construction with patience and tenacity. Neither the invasion of the soul by God, nor the 'return' of the mystics, has any resemblance of mental disintegration."

It is not easy to get rid of God. Will you read what Jung says on this subject in the *Collected Papers on Analytical Psychology*, edited by Dr. Constance E. Long:

"The concept of God is simply a necessary psychological function." The *consensus gentium* has spoken of gods for æons past, and will be speaking of them in æons to come. Beautiful and perfect as man may think his reason, he may nevertheless assure himself that is only one of the possible mental functions, coinciding merely with the corresponding side of the phenomena of the universe. All around is the irrational, that which is not congruous with reason. And this irrationalism is likewise a psychological function, namely the absolute unconscious; whilst the function of consciousness is essentially rational. Heraclitus, the ancient, that really very wise man, discovered the most wonderful of all psychological laws, namely, the *regulating function of antithesis*. He termed this "enantiodromia" (lashing together) by which he meant that at some time everything meets with its opposite. Man may not *identify* himself with reason, for he is not wholly a rational being, and never can or ever will become one. That is a fact of which every pedant of civilization should take note. What is irrational cannot and may not be stomped out. The gods cannot and may not die. Woe betide those men who have disinfected heaven with rationalism; God-Almightiness has entered into them, because they would not admit God as an absolute function. Only he escapes from the cruel law of enantiodromia who knows how to separate himself from the unconscious—not by repressing it, for then it seizes him from behind—*but by presenting it visibly to himself as something that is totally different from him....* He must learn to differentiate in his thoughts between what is the ego and what is the non-ego. The latter is the collective psyche or absolute unconscious.... In order to differentiate the psychological ego from the psychological non-ego, man must necessarily stand *upon firm feet* in his ego-function.

"Obviously the depreciation and repression of such a powerful function as that of religion has serious consequences for the psychology of the individual. One period of skepticism came to a close with the horrors of the French revolution. At the present time we are again experiencing an ebullition of the unconscious destructive powers of the collective psyche. The result is an unparalleled general slaughter. That is just what the unconscious was tending towards. This tendency had previously been inordinately strengthened by the rationalism of modern life, which by depreciating everything irrational caused the function of irrationalism to sink into the unconscious." "There is indeed no possible alternative but to acknowledge irrationalism as a psychological function that is necessary and always existent. Its results are not

21

LAST LETTERS FROM THE LIVING DEAD MAN

to be taken as concrete realities (that would involve repression), but as *psychological realities*. They are realities because they are *effective* things, that is, they are *actualities*."

So we need not be ashamed to admit that we pray! In this grim period of history, when the soul is face to face with itself and its brother as it has never been, we may speak with a greater simplicity than in the old conventionally smiling days before the war. I pray—and so do you, whoever you are, if only by groaning "Oh, God!" when you suffer. Prayer is an instinct. Even an atheist will pray, if he finds himself beyond human aid. A friend of mine who was killed at the front used to take holy communion every morning, and he was doubtless a saner and better soldier for it. One need not be a Roman Catholic to see the beauty of that act of faith.

Whether God be a "dominant of the super personal unconscious," a psychological function, or a mathematical equation, makes not the slightest difference to me. As William James would say, "He works." And whether the souls of our dead live in us, as Fechner says, or whether they are relics in the personal and collective unconscious, or whether they are "concrete realities" that can materialize by using astral and etheric substance, makes also not the slightest difference to me. If you could know how utterly I am at peace about this whole question!

And many other differences appear, on close examination, to be mainly differences of viewpoint and phraseology. The "astral world" of the Theosophists, mediaeval and modern, corresponds to a certain level of the unconscious. 'X' says in one of the *Letters* which follow, written in 1917, that melancholy may be produced by the

22

pressure of the unhappy dead who make us fear. If you locate the dead in the unconscious, which surges up in moments of passivity, the dead will have the same effect. Having given much of the leisure time of a laborious life to a study of the theories and practises of mysticism and occultism, as formulated by many different schools, I could write volumes (if I had the inclination, which I have not) in tracing out the psychological roots and the relations between these things. My own unconscious is rich with such images. Some of the most striking parallels have not been written about, so far as I know.

And Jung seems to have covered, with the wide mantle of his comprehension, even the frailties of those who believe in prophetic dreams. He says:

"The unconscious possesses possibilities of wisdom that are completely closed to consciousness, for the unconscious has at its disposal not only all the psychic contents that are under the threshold because they have been forgotten or overlooked, but also the wisdom of the experience of untold ages, deposited in the course of time and lying potential in the human brain. The unconscious is continually active, creating combinations of its materials; these serve to indicate the *future path* of the individual. It creates prospective combinations just as our consciousness does, only they are considerably superior to the conscious combinations both in refinement and extent. The unconscious may therefore be an unparalleled guide for human beings.... "The unconscious must contain all the material that has *not yet* reached the level of consciousness. These are the germs of future conscious contents."

He seems to think that true prophecies are merely

the result of synthesis by the unconscious of tendencies (*whether in the personal or universal unconscious*) significant for future occurrences. Referring to Maeterlinck's "*inconsistent supérieur,*" he says of the prophetic interpretation of dreams:

"The aversion of the exact sciences against this sort of thought process which is hardly to be called fantastic is only an *overcompensation* of the thousands of years old but all too great inclination of man to believe in soothsaying."

I am told that the hearing of voices in the hypnogogic state indicates "a slight tendency to dissociation." Very well. Probably the voices come from a deeper level than automatic writing, whatever the inspiration of automatic writing may be.

Now while the things which 'X' in the following letters advised America to do, before America came into the war, were the very things which we did *after* we came into the war and which we could not have done except as war measures, our entrance was not written down as a specific prophesy in these letters. Any startling prophecy has always had a tendency to shake me out of the passive state in which automatic writing is possible. *But*— during the weeks from February to April 1917, in the hypnogogic state preceding sleep, I several times heard, "We are coming into the war." Of course I did not write that down in the manuscript, as *it was not a part of the manuscript.* What is heard is heard, what is written is written. I merely mention it as a curious phenomenon for it was probably the synthesis of the *deeper levels* of my unconscious. It was certainly the tragic hope of my conscious mind; but the conscious alone would not have produced a voice.

If anybody wonders that I should admit hearing hypnogogic voices, I can only say that I regard these things rather objectively and impersonally. I never hear voices except when half-asleep. If my very accurate memory has not slipped a cog, William James used to talk freely of his hypnogogic experiences. The more we know about our little personalities, the less monstrously important they seem. And the "hearing of voices" has more than once played a respectable rôle in history, before and after Moses. But I do not imagine that I have any prophetic mission, nor do I feel in any hurry to "unite myself with the ocean of divinity," nor feel any impulse violently to turn my back upon the universal. There is a happy mean, which makes for efficiency in life, for health and understanding.

I have touched upon analytical psychology in this Introduction because I am so constituted that I cannot publish this last volume of my automatic writings without indicating my point of view, with the same frankness as in former Introductions. Please do not blame science because I have not lost through the analytic process my instinctive belief in individual immortality. I assure you it has not been the fault of science. If anyone objects that I have only touched the threads of this great web of psychology which lead towards the subject of this book, I can only say that this forward being by way of preface to this book, no other course was possible on account of the limitations of space and artistic relevancy.

Psychology as a method of healing I leave to the physicians, who have written many books about it, containing bibliographies. And booksellers have catalogues.

Anyone interested can write to them. This is by way of excusing myself from answering letters of enquiry. I have unselfishly and laboriously written so many hundreds of letters! Now I want to write other things. The resolution of psychological "complexes" frees energy for sublimation in work. It frees ideas for use in art. Dr. Beatrice M. Hinkle, in the introduction to her translation of Jung's *Psychology of the Unconscious*, says that "this psychology which is pervading all realms of thought ... seems destined to be a psychological-philosophical system for the understanding and practical advancement of human life."

So, having found a well whose waters were refreshing, I note the fact—and pass on. The train of thought which the reader has followed in this Introduction is the train of thought which led me—after some delay—to the publication of the book. I am glad that these *Last Letters from the Living Dead Man* are a call to courage, to restraint, to faith in the great and orderly future of America and the world, a call to all those positive qualities so gravely needed in these days of the rebuilding of Peace.

For I do not believe that Bolshevism, or any other form of lunacy, will find foothold in the United States. A nation with universal suffrage, for man and woman, certainly has no incentive for a resort to insane destruction. In the last State campaign it was interesting to watch the reactions of women to the privileges and duties of suffrage. I watched it only in one party, the Democratic, but it was doubtless everywhere the same. There was an added dignity, a sense of new responsibility, and always courtesy and real fellowship among the women and the men. Its happening to correspond in time with the Fourth Liberty Loan campaign, and the printing of casualty lists, made it all the more significant. No, these level-headed, socially responsible women will never be swept away by collective insanity; and as the men who return from the front will return to these women, their mothers, wives and sisters, I do not think that we shall lose in peace what we have gained in war.

And now—remembering always that this book was written between February 1917, and February 1918—you may read the *Last Letters from the Living Dead Man*.

ELSA BARKER

NEW YORK, EASTER DAY, 1919.

LETTER 1

The Genius of America

February 3, 1917

I WANT TO WRITE OF America, land of my latest birth, land of the future. Great is the road that the Genius of America may travel, and her feet have already passed the early stages of it. The Genius of America! Each land is watched over and its children guided—guided and moved—by a Genius. Would you feel the Genius of America, go alone into the woods at night, watch and listen and invoke. Perhaps the answer may come, its recognition of you, your recognition of it.

If you are one of those who can hear the words which the Great Ones speak in the silence; perhaps you will hear something with the ears of your soul. If so, do not hasten to divulge the message, but treasure it in your heart; for that which is treasured in the heart can sometimes be felt and understood by the hearts of others. If you are one of those who will serve willingly, the secret of your heart may be shared in silence with those who can hear in the silence. The hour approaches when the mission of this land may be manifested. The hour approaches when the Genius of this land shall force its will upon this land. That will not be an easy task. So many wills have sought to wrest the reins from the guiding hand; so many eyes, looking in so many directions, have seen so many goals. But there is one will so strong that it can, when its hour is come, gather up the wills of men as a strong wind gathers a mass of loosely lying straws and sweeps them along.

You know not the power of a will that has God behind it. You know not the power of a purpose that has God behind it and the future before it. Those who get in the way of the Genius of this land will be broken, like straws that would resist the wind. I have watched from my unseen place the labors of many. I have helped unseen with my faith to strengthen the hearts of many. I shall wait now unseen till the act of destiny is accomplished. You who have followed me from my first gropings in the twilight of the new life, before the clearness came; you who have followed me on my journeys among the battlefields, both in and above the world, follow me yet a little further, with your minds ajar for the entrance of the truth I have to tell you, the advice I have to give you. For my advice is disinterested as the rain, and my truth is offered as freely as the light.

I have come a long way since I laid down my body a few brief years ago, years of crowded brevity, in which the world has moved as fast as I, and sometimes with more pain. For he who knows the purpose of his pain can bear it better than the child who knows only that he suffers. I should have spoken to you before, but you would not let me. Child! Would you stand in the way with your personal wishes, and your shrinkings that are also wishes of a negative kind? Blocked by your will to avoid this labor, I sought another entrance; but it was too much encumbered by prejudices and preconceived ideas, and all the litter of mental fragments that had accumulated through years of residence in a creed-bound place. You who have dwelt but briefly in many tents have no obstructions at your door, save such as are placed by your will, and those I now sweep away. I shall pass in and out, and speak to you as I choose.

LETTER 2

Fear Not

February 8, 1917

DID I NOT TELL YOU many months ago that
the soul of Abraham Lincoln kept watch above
this land that he died to save from disruption,
and that he would keep vigil until America should have
passed through her next great trial? You questioned then
what that trial would be. Do you question now? And yet
you do not know. Slowly the months have gone by, reced-
ing into the past. You saw in vision the German Emperor
in spiked helmet standing opposite to Uncle Sam in his
shirt-sleeves, did you not suppose that it would come to
this? You are wise to keep such visions to yourself.

Do not fancy that this war will end without greater
changes than the world has ever known before. When I
told you nearly two years ago that the battle between the
powers of good and evil had been won in the invisible
regions, I knew because my Teacher told me so; but do
not believe that the new age can dawn without greater
trouble and greater changes than you can now imagine.
Birth is change and birth is painful, and birth is bloody
and exhausting. The pains that have gone before are only
the pains of labor. The stars in their courses fight for the
new race.

I have written of the bloody fields of Europe. Now
I would write of America and her future, her near and
her far future; for the sun is approaching the Eastern

horizon and the dawn clouds are already tinged with the coming day. America, do not despair! Your destiny is assured. In the storms to come, think of the freshness after the storm, when the ground shall smell sweet and birds shall sing. For the birds will sing to the children of the new age. In the midst of changes there will come a lull. The world will say, "It is over, the old things will return, and all will be as before." But nothing will ever be exactly as it was before. In the lull you shall draw breath, and make ready for other changes. Yes, many things will be changed, even the hearts of men.

The world has known terror. Without experience of terror, without the poise that comes from the facing of terror undaunted, the world could not face the future without failure. Is there anything now, after thirty months of war that could surprise the world? Is there anything that the world could not face? Oh, remember that you are immortal, and that you who go out of life will come back again, strengthened by the rest in the invisible! For a change of place is a rest of consciousness. To those whose nerves are weary, wise doctors prescribe a change. A rest in the invisible worlds is more refreshing than a summer in the mountains. Do not fear death. I passed through death, and I am more rested now than a strong man in the morning. I would not go back to my old body. When I want a body again I shall build a new one. I know the process of building, having built so many before.

Be joyous with me. A wise man once said that only the unendurable is tragic. The world, and the souls of the world, can endure the change that is coming. Have not wars prepared them for it? That is why wars had to be. America is rich. Her vaults are full of gold, her mines are full of ore, and her fresh soil is full of richness. Shall she fear a future in which labor can procure all things for the body, and faith can procure all things for the soul? The history of this land is a history of faith. Did not Columbus start across the trackless ocean, led only by the star of his faith? Did not your ancestors follow, led by their faith in the future? The past has gone back to God, it is safe as a dead man; but the future is coming to you, and your faith shall make it sure.

Fear naught. In the early days of this land your forefathers slept in quiet, though the red man lurked in the forest, and hunger lurked in the failure of harvests, and men and children could only be winter-warm when trees had been felled for fuel. Now you fear famines of coal? The earth is heavy with coal. You fear famines of wheat, when your muscles grow fat for lack of exercise. They who came first to this land had varied reasons for fear, but you have no reasons for fear. Labor is sweet. The child who makes labor of play can vouch for the truth of that saying. Can you not then make play of your labor? When I was a child I built houses of blocks. I longed to be building. I dug ditches in the garden. I made boats of chips and sailed them on a puddle. I planted seeds.

And learning? In the libraries of the world and in the brains of men is stored the learning of the ages. The new age will not lack the archives of all ages. Though paper is less enduring than parchment, it will last over into the new age. Fear not. By hints I convey to your mind that many changes will come. What then? All progress is change. Go out with it to meet the future, with a smile on your face and a song on your lips. The future wears a rose in its buttonhole, as your Vagrom Angel would say.

The Promise of Spring

February 17, 1917

WHEN YOU LEARN to think of life as a whole, of which you are a part containing in yourself the potentialities of the whole, then you will look upon these great changes with joy. The One must sometimes sacrifice itself to itself, and by elimination secure a new lease of life. The whole—call it the race, or the earth-spirit, or what you will—may grow too fat and lazy, as a man may grow too large to move about with ease, and then by war among the organs, by fever, fasting or remedies, the equilibrium is restored, and he starts again a new man, ready to face the future.

Grim, does it seem? But who told you that the purposes of life were always smiling? In the deeps of the earth and in the deeps of man are dark substances. The cold of winter is a hardship for those who expose themselves to the elements; but winter is the ebb tide of that changing sea of life whose flood-tide is the summer. Rhythm, always rhythm. I would not have you discouraged by the winter of the race, for the spring will come and the roses will bloom again. March winds! They are followed by April showers and May flowers. We are now in February. When the skies are dark and the snows fall, we gather round the fire and think of the future, when the flowers shall bloom again and green grass shall cover the earth and birds shall sing in the trees. The sun "crosses the line" in March when the winds blow, and enters the sign of the Ram, and the Zodiac is traversed again by the great life-giver the Sun. Do you shiver and grow afraid when the Equinox approaches?

The soul, too, has its winter of materialism and its ideal spring. I have looked at the world from the outside, and I see no cause for despair. I have looked at the soul from the inside, and I see great cause for rejoicing. You look forward to the end of the war, but the soul must battle to the end of its journey. So long as the soul is cased in matter there will be wars enough, for the greatest struggles are the soul's struggles with itself. I have told you this before. Sometimes it goes out to fight, sometimes it goes in; the sword will not rust in the scabbard.

Think less of yourself and think more of the race. You lose the vision of the whole by regarding too closely the parts, by regarding too closely yourself that is only one of the parts. Think of yourself as the race, and think of the race as yourself; then yourself becomes the race, and the race becomes yourself; "the Universe grows I." There was once a God so great that the cells of his body were minor gods. You may become so great that the cells of your body will be glad to sacrifice themselves to your welfare. By renouncing the will to live, you may make yourself immortal. By renouncing the will to joy, you may become joyous. Once I desired to become a great man. Now when I only desire that Man shall be great, I have increased in stature myself.

Once I desired to be loved; but now when I love for love's sake and not for my own sake, I am loved by a multitude. Surely I found my life by losing it, and the words of the Master were justified. I look down at the world as

I once looked down at my garden. I see that the grass is sprouting and I know that seeds are in the ground. I have planted seeds in the hearts of men that shall germinate and reach up towards the sunshine, for I had faith in the spring. For a while I have left Europe to itself, and have come back to the land that I love best. I have journeyed from State to State, and have watched the wills of our legislators. They too are aware that a Force is at work through them. They feel the responsibility of their place; they feel themselves as moving parts of the great whole whose name is America. The Flag is a symbol of their consecration.

I have walked in the woods, where the spirits of the land fore-gather for counsels which the newspapers do not report. They too are aware of their consecration. They strengthen you with their faith. When I lived as a man in America I did not know America. To know the meaning of home we must wander. I am all for unity now. Do not let yourself be weakened by fear of the parts. America is a whole, and as a whole she must work. To fuse these many races together is the mission of the present hour. Do not lend your hearts to division. I see a great leader of men who shall arise from this land. His mission will be the union of races. He will be a teacher and a prophet.

The Diet of Gold

March 10, 1917

T HE VERY INFLUENCES that now tend to disrupt this country will later draw it together. The many will find their meeting point in the One. That idea of national unity must be fostered, even to the extent of patient tolerance of racial temperaments. Those who are in the process of being separated from their old race and amalgamated with the new race, feel the strain of the change. It irritates them and their blood protests, even when their wills bid them forge new bonds for themselves. Few "hyphenated Americans" would be willing to go bodily back to their old allegiance.

America is the most interesting of all countries, and we who see it from this side of the airy frontier see it in historical perspective. The view that is nearest to our point of view is that of your present Chief Executive. His eyes are far seeing. He anticipates the clearer sight that will one day be his, when he has finished his work. Our country is suffering this moment, in March, of the year of our Lord nineteen hundred and seventeen, from an indigestion of gold. You have swallowed more gold than you can assimilate, and your organs are congested. If to restore the equilibrium, some of this gold should be regurgitated, by war or by other means, do not in the weariness that follows fancy that the nation is going to die.

Do not be shocked by my figures of speech. I want

to get into your consciousness an understanding of facts and conditions as they exist. You cannot feed on gold. "Gold is a medium of exchange." When it is merely hoarded it has lost its relation to life. A miser nation is a sadder subject for contemplation than a miser man, to secure himself from the dangers of the future by amassing gold for its own sake. A miser nation may think that by amassing gold for its own sake it can save itself from the financial dangers threatening the world after these years of war. But the miser, known as such, is in danger of being robbed and murdered. And the miser nation is in danger of being attacked and looted by other nations.

You Americans want to be generous to the homeless and foodless people of Europe; but your generosity has not yet deprived of one square meal the hundred-million-headed being that is America. I do not care so much what you do with your gold. But I care much what you do with your food. You are not alchemists that you can make gold potable. You are humans with delicate stomachs. Even a hen will not lay eggs for you unless she is well fed. If she protests, you can punish her by eating her; but the luckiest break of her wishbone will not produce for you another hen. Better conserve her labor power by gifts of grain, and have your eggs for breakfast and for hatching. She has periods of laziness when she wants to set still; but put a few of her own eggs under her, and watch for results. Later I shall tell you of other but no less practical ways of ensuring a supply of breakfasts.

LETTER 5

Contingent Fees

March 10, 1917

TODAY I HEARD that a certain rich man (unmindful of the camel and the needle's eye), supposing that the letters from this Living Dead Man had been profitable to you, that there was "money in them," was considering the question whether he should financially back a medium who stood ready to declare that she was in communication with me, that I repudiated the books written through you, and stood sponsor for certain manuscripts written "through" her, as my only genuine messenger to the world.

I join in your laughter, at your supposed "profitable" investment in the securities of the other world, and at the eagerness to get aboard a sea-of-ether-worthy ship exhibited by people who have not paid their fare. I may as well tell you now that this country and some others are scattered over with supposed "communications" from me. It would seem that my writing arms are as numerous as the feet of a centipede. It would also seem by the style of some of these supposed communications, that I have as many minds as Indra has eyes. Even the elements of the ouija board do not contradict themselves so frequently as these amanuenses make me contradict myself. I think you will have to trademark me.

After the serious nature of my recent letters, it relaxes

me to jest. If you include this letter in the book, please head it "Contingent".

LETTER 6

The Three Appeals

March 11, 1917

I STAND OUTSIDE THE world and look inside the hearts of men. I see more than I saw when I was a man among them. Had I then looked as deep into my own heart as I now look into theirs, I should have seen the hearts of my fellow beings reflected in my own, for we differ from one another as one insect differs from another. There are differences between insects.

I look into your hearts, O men! And this is what I see: Ideals and hypocrisy, self interest and altruism, hunger and satiety. Shall I, in offering advice, appeal to your ideals, your self interest, or your hunger? The opposite three would never spur you to action along the lines I would have you spurred.

LETTER 7

The Builders

March 22, 1917

I HAVE PROMISED TO offer you advice as to how you may restore your equilibrium. Use much of this superfluity of gold in rebuilding devastated Europe. Give her credits and give her food. You, who can work in the fields, raise food to feed Europe. You, who can build, give the labor of your hands wherever it is needed. You, who are discontented here, go back to that Europe which gave you birth. By so doing you will give yourselves a new point of view, and you will give yourselves a new interest. A new interest is a new lease on life.

Make sacrifices. In saying that, I have two objects in view, the effect on the world and the effect on yourselves. To work for the ideal is sometimes more practical than to work for what is called the real. When I tell you to rebuild Europe, you can take it as ideal advice or practical advice, depending on your point of view. It is ideal because Europe needs rebuilding; it is practical because just now and for a time to come America needs to get her mind on something outside herself. We give that advice to individuals when they are too self-centered. There is so much discontent and so much uncertainty that anything which can catch and hold the attention of masses of men, which can make them forget themselves, may enable them to be used by the Genius of the race, which works for the welfare of the race as a whole.

Lend your money to Europe, and do not ask usurious interest. Yes, you can take interest, for money has earning power, and the laborer—even the laborer Gold—is worthy of his hire. But help by your generous lendings at low interest to lessen the awful burden of taxation for the people of Europe, which makes also for discontent and discouragement. Go to Europe, many of you, that you may see what war does to a country, what it might do to your country should you selfishly expose yourselves to a desire on the part of outsiders to take from you by force that which you have so skilfully acquired. Go, that you may see and feel, as you can only see and feel face to face, the spirit of self-sacrifice and national devotion which has animated the people of Europe in this long war. They have found their souls, but you have not yet found your soul.

There are engineers in this country who are less needed here than they will be needed in Europe. There are specialists in all the branches of science who are more needed there than here. We have specialists enough. We can spare a few of them. Build ships. Build more ships. Keep the men occupied. Give them an objective. Do not let them brood. An idle brain is the devil's workshop. If you have not work enough, make work. There are things enough to be done. Build ships. Now in regard to your management of railroads and other public utilities. The day for government control was heralded when the threat of a strike came that would have, if put into effect, blocked the wheels of a nation. All those public utilities whose blocked wheels could threaten the national life and the movements of men should be managed by the government. This is not socialism, or any other *ism*. You, who have stock in them, do not take alarm. A way can be found that will satisfy you.

Think of the good of the whole, for you who are a part cannot prosper without the welfare of the whole. This is not cant. It is a sort of race biology. I look down and see you as a great being, and I prescribe for you as a being, a race-unity, not as a few individuals here and there. The cells in the body of the race-being must all be working together. Get a unit of consciousness, as a race. Yield yourselves to the consciousness of the race-unit. Be as individual as you please, but be individual parts. Get into balance with other individuals, positive and negative.

Make the rebuilding of Europe an objective point. Make it possible for many discontented workers to go to work in Europe. You may say that the armies of Europe, when released from military service, will furnish workers enough; but there cannot be too many. There is a double object in this: the object of getting work done, and that of the psychological effect upon the worker. I wish I could get into your minds by infusion the state of consciousness that is mine. I wish I could make you see that separation is death and that unity is life. I have spoken of government control of railroads, but that is only the beginning. There should be governmental handling of food. Begin gradually, one thing after another. It is the destiny of the world to go in that direction. You cannot block the wheels of that chariot.

Serve if you hope to survive would be a good motto. You cannot survive if you do not serve—all of you. I like that figure of the cell which is a part of the race-being. It is the way I see you.

Just a word about nervous diseases. Yes, it is related to what I have been saying. When at last the let-up comes after the unnatural strain of war, the minds of men in going back, or in attempting to go back to their normal state, may find themselves unable immediately to adjust to the changed conditions. For a long time the brains of men and women have been stimulated by the coffee of concerted action; when they are thrown back on themselves they may relax too much. Or, on the other hand, an unnatural excitement may drive them into all kinds of excesses. Have you ever seen victims of mania who could not rest, who had lost the ability to rest? They walk up and down, and drum with their feet, and clench their hands. So many men and women may be, after this war. There is certain to be an excess of love excitement, and work is a good panacea for that complaint.

Then again, after years of war, years in which many have not known in the morning whether they would be alive at night, they may retain the habit of dread. They may fear to rest and fear to relax. Thus they may welcome any excitement, as a substitute for the stimulus to which they have been accustomed. That is another reason why I would send Americans to labor with the laborers of Europe. Not that the American working man is phlegmatic, far from it; but with his mind unaccustomed to fear anything, except the loss of his job and consequent hunger, he will have an effect of confidence and hope on those around him. The American likes to feel that he is leading, and in what better way can he indulge that propensity than in leading his associates to hope?

You have no idea—you cannot have an idea—of the great depression that will follow this war for a short while. It will be the relaxation, the letting go. Always after war the ebb tide is followed by great activity; but it is that ebb tide which we have to consider. You in America will feel it. You have become accustomed to seeing gold flow towards these shores. When the stream lessens, you will have to combat the tendency to fear that lessening. Panics are like personal fear, intensified by mass. The world is drawing close together, and what influences a part influences the whole.

After the war will also come an opening of the psychic senses of men, everywhere. This, while good in itself, may become an added danger. Prophets, true and false, will arise everywhere, with many remedies for the diseases of souls and of bodies. If I may make another suggestion, it would be that those who have psychic awakening should think twice before proclaiming the fact. It is a new sense that is coming into manifestation; but as the opening of the eyes in an early stage of evolution probably revealed as many dangers as blessings, so the new sense will reveal dangers. Do not try to close the new sense, but do not be carried away by it. Remember that it will be practically general, and like every new sense it will be defective for a long time. It will reveal false things as well as true. If a man opened his eyes for the first time upon a harmless tree, he might mistake it for a monster.

Restraint in all things, moderation in all things, even in the laudable desire to action. Weigh and measure. Prove before accepting anything—prove by reason and by intuition if you cannot wait for proof by practise. Weigh and measure what I say, as well as what the wildest new prognosticator says. Discourage hysteria. A wave of hysteria is likely to sweep over the world. As revolution follows revolution, the startled inhabitants of the world may tell themselves that nothing in the universe is stable, that all is going to destruction, and that as they cannot save themselves from what seems to be universal chaos, they may as well get all the pleasurable excitement possible out of the passing moment. Restraint, restraint!

I see women afraid to bear children because of the uncertainty of the morrow. I see men afraid to marry because of the uncertainty of domesticity. I see farmers hesitate to plant because of the uncertainty of the harvest. Again I say, be not afraid. If you sow, you shall reap. If you marry, you shall build a home. If you have children, the race will protect them—and you are a part of the race. Restraint! Fearlessness!

LETTER 8

The World of Mind

March 24, 1917

I WISH THAT MORE people of sane, sound mind would experiment in telepathic communication. I know there is any amount of uncoordinated and half serious playing with phenomena; but with scientific accuracy of observation and scientific precision in recording data, not only the body of sensible literature on these subjects would be increased, but the habits of careful observation and precision in reporting supernormal facts would be developed in the experimentalists. You who write for me, continue to make and record experiments. You are almost too cautious, but most persons are not cautious enough.

Explain the necessary conditions of passivity and activity between those working together. Though the best results are often obtained by you alone, yet the testimony of one person is not so convincing as the testimony of several who have witnessed and taken part in the same phenomena. But you are right in hesitating to take on the psychic conditions of insincere and merely curious people who would like to work with you. The great difficulty with most persons is that they cannot make themselves sufficiently negative *for the time being*. When the experiments are over they can and should become equally positive. They can shift from one pole to the other, and they must do so if they wish to preserve their physical health and balance.

But bear in mind that the influences from this side are good and bad, even as the influences in the world are; and if you feel that any "presence" is hostile, at once banish it and become positive. After any approach by an undesirable influence, you should not for some hours let yourself become negative. Go for a walk, or attack some difficult piece of work, or read a book that demands mental activity in order to grasp its meaning. You live in a sea of mind, as well as in a psychic sea; they interpenetrate, and they interpenetrate with the physical; but in working through and with them, keep them as distinct as possible. I work more and more in the mental world, and less and less in the astral; but the majority of my readers will not know exactly what I mean by that statement. There is a greater difference between the astral and the mental plane than there is between the astral and the physical.

Do not despise the astral. Its dynamics are of colossal import. But cultivate more and more the purely mental, because the astral in all of you is developed beyond the mental. Those who learn that they can create in mind need to develop a sense of responsibility. They are too reckless in demonstrating their power. Remember that as you go up in the planes of being you get into subtler and subtler regions, and strength increases with the degree of subtlety—not the reverse, as you would naturally suppose.

One of the greatest temptations of the mental world is that of the creation of falsehoods. By stating that which is not true, you project into the realm of mind a picture that has a certain permanency. It may deceive others, but in time it will deceive you, its creator. Those who speak falsely cannot perceive truth. Those who create false pictures in the mental world will be deceived by those very pictures; they will reap the effects of the causes they have set up. Have you not known people who were always being deceived by their "friends"? They are generally those who have left deceiving pictures behind themselves. There are people who cannot discriminate between the false and the true. They deceive and are deceived. Those who deceive are always deceived, whatever their supposed intellect may be.

And I would say to those to whom I now suggest experiments with clairvoyance and telepathy, that if they have planted the seeds of falsehood they will reap a harvest of deceptive appearances. Test yourself in that way, you who believe yourselves to be sincere. You may learn something of value regarding your own karma. (Yes, I will use Theosophical or Indian terms when they express my meaning. Those who rewrite the Oriental philosophies in western terms can pass for original only with the ignorant.) What the new race needs most of all is truth. Modern science is preparing the world for the fearless facing of truth. The man who toils over a microscope that he may observe and record some *fact* in nature, is more the servant of God than the man who with sanctimonious face tells his fellow creatures what they must *not* do; for his work at least is positive in its results.

There are too many "thou shalt nots" and too few "I shalls". The new race will develop a wide tolerance. It will discourage undesirable things more by ignoring them than by attacking them. By attacking a thing we give it power. Work more and more in the world of mind. The results in the physical will be immense.

America's Good Friday

April 6, 1917

I**T IS PAST MIDNIGHT.** It is Good Friday. Momentous decisions for the world and for all time are heavy in the souls of men. On the day that this day stands for, in the long ago, a man (who was also a god) stood forth alone for the ideas of love and human brotherhood. At last, after all these years, the thing for which he died may be realized. But there was a crucifixion on that Friday, centuries ago.

I have brought you from a faraway shore that you might witness a great struggle in the souls of men. You have arrived at a center. Today, in thousands of churches throughout Christendom, prayers will be offered to the godman who died that the god in man might live. Today in millions of hearts the cross will be set up. It is so still here at midnight, at a few minutes past midnight on this day of days. Christianity has arisen, and presses forward to Golgotha to witness an event. Pray! Prayer is the affirmation by the soul of its unity with the One. War is the affirmation of the soul of its separateness from many. Love your enemies. It is the only way that you can conquer them.

LETTER 10

The Crucible

April 12, 1917

L ET US SPEAK A little of this initiation through which the race is passing. Always the trials precede the attainment. When these wars are over there will be a new world, for the souls of men will have been baptized with the fire and the blood. America must have her part in it. To her also must come the trials and the attainment. Watch and pray. Some day I will send you back to commune with the soul of the Old World— some day we will send you back. It is another Europe you will find, a Europe tried by fire, and some of it will be fine steel, and some of it will be clinkers in the furnace, for the fire proves the metal, and separates the metal from the slag.

From before the war to this day, the battles of the earth have been enacted also in your soul, the blood and the fire, the pain and the travail. You too have passed through the fiery furnace. Long ago, when you identified your soul with the soul of the world, you took upon yourself the trials of the world, the initiatory trials. You also called down upon yourself the weight of your old karma, the effects of the causes you had set up through the ages. That you are at rest for a time means only that you have worked yourself free from a little of the load. Had you not done it now, you would have had to do it in the future. Rejoice for every trial that brings you nearer to the goal. And this I say for all men.

If I speak of the world now, instead of that part only that we call America, it is to identify the part with the whole. If I speak of you personally, it is to identify you with the whole. Back in that Europe to which you will go, you will find two classes, those who have become fine steel, and those who have become refuse. You will know the one from the other.

They will welcome you back, for you have passed through the fire with them. They will welcome your country, too, for it now turns its face to the fire. Be not discouraged by dismal prophecies. Man does not live by bread alone. If you have less to eat, your bodies will grow finer. If you have more to do, your minds and spirits will expand. Few of you work to your full capacity. The unit of force that is man may generate much energy, drawing it up from the deeps of himself at the call of need or of will.

Work harder now. Once I told you to rest more, but the laborers are called to the vineyard. The hour of rest will come again, when the day draws near its close. In entering into the war, my country, put away all rancor, and fight for the right in which there is no rancor. Hate not. The hour for hate is past. (I say this, knowing that Hate and Fear, the mother of Hate, will come and challenge your souls.) I do not hate, and I do not fear, and I shall stay with you until the day draws to its close. Are you sorry now that you let me speak again? When fear comes to your house, I will speak to you of courage. When hate shall menace you, I will turn it into love. I have found the Philosopher's Stone that can transmute base metals into gold.

Hate will be turned to love in this land where the Eagle cries. Listen to the cry of the Eagle. It is a free bird, and it flies high. Its message has only been hinted at, in the years that have yet been numbered. The Eagle will teach freedom. They will listen—across the sea. America is indeed the melting pot of nations. I can find no better figure of speech. The German-American who is loyal to America now, who hides the tragedy in his heart behind a brave face, may also come through the furnace fine steel. I am glad you know that they suffer. Hold the loyal ones in your heart, with all other loyal Americans. So you will help in the process of melting. To some of them the tragedy will open the doors of initiation. Their loyalty to a pledge is a finer trial than the fire of a battlefield. Those who are loyal must not be made pariahs. Of those who are disloyal I say nothing, but leave them to the Law.

The initiatory process! It has the earth in its grasp. There are those whom you love that it has in its grasp, too. They suffer, as you have suffered. But they shall find peace.

Make Clean Your House

May 4, 1917

DO YOU KNOW THAT the human race is being weighed in the balances? Work and pray that it may not be found wanting. We who dwell in the clear light of that world which is to you the Other World, can see the handwriting on the wall. The world has been too dishonest. In an honest world, could this war have been? In the world that is to come, nation will not distrust nation, nor man distrust man. But now distrust is a necessary part of the human equipment. You may trust—but not too far. You may love your neighbor—but not too much. You may do to your brother as you would have him do to you—but not all the time.

America was built on a foundation of ideals; but there is too much of the mud of personal seeking mixed with the good clay of your bricks. You washed away with your blood one plague spot, that of slavery; but there is another plague spot you have got to wash away. Will you do it with the free water of good will, or will you do it again with your blood? I wait to see. Do not say that the world's troubles are over, because America has come into the war. The world's troubles are not over. When the war is over—the greater war—make clean your house, O America! There is no other civilized country where the premiums upon dishonesty are so high.

Can you buy a pound of butter and be certain that

you get sixteen full ounces? Can you buy a pound of meat and be sure that the scales are true? A new race is being born. Begin with those children, and teach them honesty before you teach them geography—honesty with the parents, honesty with each other, honesty with themselves. "As the twig is bent the tree inclines." When I was a little boy I was taught that George Washington could not tell a lie. I had an ideal of George Washington. I wanted to emulate him. And so when I was a man I sought truth. I looked for it on the surface of the ground, and also in deep wells. Once I spent years in the wilderness trying to find truth in myself. I remained in the wilderness until I found it. Had I not found it, I should have left my bones there.

You need a new set of copybook maxims. If the boy who writes "Honesty is the best policy" at school in the morning, sees in the afternoon his father trying to trade a balky horse for a good roadster, he wonders if his teacher is fooling him. The disillusionment of children is tragic with menace for the coming State. I would rather see reproach in the eyes of an Adept Teacher than in the eyes of a child. If I fail my teacher I do not hurt him seriously, if I fail my child I hurt him irreparably. You must face the fact that the life of America is going to be reorganized. You have wondered why I have not written of late. I have been busy, studying America. I have seen much that I can tell you, and much that I cannot tell you—yet. For I want you to be quiet. You could not be quiet if you knew as much as I know.

It has been said that necessity knows no law. Forget it not, you war-profiteers who would corner the world's necessities. Remember that a cornered animal is dangerous, and a cornered necessity has hoofs and horns. There is a disease that has no name among the doctors—the disease of colossal possessions. Its symptoms are a voracious appetite for more possessions, and a phobia lest possessions be lost. It is worse than neuralgia and indigestion combined to disturb the rest of the victim. I long to see a hundred million and more people living in peace and plenty in America.

Fanatics prattle about the confiscation of great fortunes. I do not care so much what you do with your fortunes. But I care much what you do with your land and your food, and I care more what you do with your men and women and little children. Do not get into a panic, I pray you. A panic is worse than a quicksand to get into. Keep calm. The country is in no danger, if it does not lose its head.

Level Heads

May 15, 1917

DO NOT GET EXCITED, you Americans. If you keep your heads, you will come through this all right. If you lose your heads, you may lose much besides—you may lose more than you can win back in a hundred years. I am not excited. I have not lost my head. (Yes, I still have a head, and hands and feet. If I should try to live out here without hands and feet, the adjustment to that unaccustomed condition would have a reactionary effect upon my head. I am not experimenting in the elimination of my members.)

You see a country now, Russia, that is making the experiment of living without its head. No nation can continue as a nation without a head, and a level one. Even the most extremely republican, democratic, socialistic, or any other kind of a nation must have a head. A completely anarchistic aggregation of people could not be called a nation. Its land would be only a geographical section populated with units, and such units unrelated to other units might as well be ciphers. Do not be impatient because I write seldom at present. I am rather busy. I shall always come when I have something that must be said. A change is coming in America. Quite a change has already come about, has it not?

This country is great, this country is strong, this country is adaptable. It can adjust itself to change. The people of this country have not been slaves for a long time. The people of Russia have been so many kinds of slaves that their reaction to freedom is unexpected by a free world. Wait! Do not lose your heads about this matter.

I do not object to there being a few persons who know that I am writing with you again. They cannot affect me, save to encourage me with their interest.

LETTER 13

Trees and Brick Walls

May 16, 1917

YOU FEAR LEST THE dismal prophesies of world disaster, of cataclysm, of the destruction of half the human race which you hear from many sources, may tend to discourage the world. Remember that hope springs eternal in the human breast. And if the minds of men are familiar with the idea of cataclysm, they will more readily adjust themselves to lesser changes. Read the Old Testament. The most dismal prophecies were not verified, but changes came.

Some of the "independent ministers" of America are more violent than Jeremiah. But they help indirectly—in accustoming the minds of men to the idea of change. If panics come—and they may—refuse to be panic-stricken. If violence comes—and it may—refuse to be violent. If discouragements come—and they will—refuse to be discouraged. When your brains become overheated, look steadily at the trees. They will quiet you. If there are no trees in your neighborhood, why, look at a brick wall in moments of excitement. A brick wall is a soothing spectacle. It stands steady, unless moved from without.

LETTER 14

Invisible Armies

May 23, 1917

MANY OF THE SOLDIERS out here who have become fully awake and self-conscious are striving to bring about those ends for which they gave their lives on earth. There are thus soldiers working on both sides of the war and on this side of the veil. Immediately after the change many of them fight each other; but they soon learn that they can do more effective work by giving attention to their comrades in the flesh. They can soothe and inspire and instruct.

We are forming an army out here. There is no lack of recruits. America must be saved, and few of you know how much America has to be saved from. But we know—we who have watched the world for the last two years and three quarters. It is not so terrible to die. It is really far more terrible to be born. The army that we are recruiting here is made up of men of all ages—all ages in this life, I mean. Yes, there are women also in our army. There are some veterans of the Civil War and veterans of the War with Spain. Over the regiments and divisions of this army there are commanders, as over the armies of earth. Otherwise the work would lack unity of purpose. Ours is mostly a volunteer army, though conscription is not unknown among us.

You wonder what I mean? Do you not suppose that we can call a soul from a useless occupation and give him useful labor? We can and do, daily. We have even recruited largely from the old and native Americans, the red skinned hunters and warriors who remain in such large numbers in the neighborhood of the earth. There is work which they only can do. There are many kinds of work and a great variety of workers. I come and go, from coast to coast. I know what is doing on the shores of the Pacific, in the Atlantic States, on the Gulf of Mexico, and the Middle and Rocky Mountain States are familiar ground to me. I am renewing my youth in this period of activity. I am working for my country. I am training, too.

Why do you smile? There is a training of the mind and the will that is more effective than any training of the physical body—quicker and more effective. Then too the astral body can be trained to a high degree of efficiency and elasticity. Surely I need not tell you this. And I am training others. We old fellows can be very useful in a time like this. I am glad now that I came out *when* I did, that I went through with my novitiate while the world was still at peace and there was leisure for many things which now I should not have time for. I had a delightful holiday. I hunted through the wilds of the invisible, and fished in the waters of space; but now I am back at my work again.

The Weakest Link

June 2, 1917

T HERE ARE IN THE archives of the Masters of Wisdom certain data relative to the past and future of this country which would make interesting reading could they be published in the newspapers at this time of national crisis. America is aware of her mission of democracy; but she is not aware of another mission equally potent—that of making the world safe for spiritual culture. I do not mean religion, as the word is ordinarily used; but I mean the culture of the spirit of love—such ideas of love as the world has inadequately grasped from the teachings of Jesus of Nazareth, grasped and let fall again because those ideas were too warm to be comfortably held by hands cooled in the material labors of selfishness.

America has laid up for herself in the regions beyond the physical a debt—an obligation that is not by any means a treasure in heaven, but which, when the debt is paid, may be a real spiritual treasure. I refer to the armies of souls who once occupied this land as free owners, and who were expelled and disinherited by the expanding civilization which grew up in the place of wigwam and hunting ground.

Those souls, many of them, desire to return. Many have already returned, and unless some way is open to them to live again the free life to which they were accustomed in the past, they will tend to become a destructive force. They cannot be eliminated so easily now, when they wear white bodies and claim citizenship with you. They are scattered from shore to shore of this wide land. You can tell them by their eagle eyes and their high cheek bones, by their free gait and love of freedom. They are hard to restrain in factory and counting house. They are clerks with a difference and laborers with a dream. Many of them have found entrance into the sunlit world as the children of European immigrants, for they find it easier to enter the blood of certain other races than the blood of the Anglo-Saxon, for all the Anglo-Saxon love of freedom.

A time may come when these now foreign-blooded primitive Americans will instinctively rebel against the restraining influences that have held them, when they will seek to live over again the old life of nature, even though they have to take it as the kingdom of heaven is said to have been taken. There is coming a time when love will be needed in this land as it has never been needed before, when "live and let live" must become a law as well as a phrase. Those who long for freedom with Nature can be given that freedom. Conditions may be hard in the great cities. I am not trying to instill fear into the American heart. On the contrary, I am trying to insure you against fear. Not long could the wheels of civilization stop turning. But they could stop—for a wink of the Cosmic Eye. America is going to be saved, and saved in the hour of her greatest danger. What will her greatest danger be? You must think that out for yourself.

Learn to see through the eye of the Planetary Spirit. Your view is too narrow. Where your library stands on shelves is for you the center of things; but the center of things is in the heart, and hearts are everywhere. If you think about the race and not about yourself, your heart will be magnified; you will see with the eyes of the heart, and he who sees with the eyes of the heart is wiser than historians or intellectual prophets. The world must be made safe for love. All men must be provided for in the scheme of the future, all men and women and little children. It is not safe to disregard any, for a chain is as strong as its weakest link, and every link must be made strong.

LETTER 16

A Council in the Forest

O NE NIGHT, TO REPOSE my soul from the labors I had undertaken, I retired to a pine forest upon the earth, in one of the New England States. Thinking to be alone, I had sought the place; but no sooner had I drifted into meditation than a strange sound fell upon my ears. It was not like the sounds of earth, it was subtler yet more penetrating; and I knew that I was listening to a song (if you may call it a song) by some of my fellow sojourners in the region beyond the sunlight.

Suddenly with a rush they leaped past me into the clearing, and forming in a circle, they waited. Then I saw a light that was not of earthly origin, the light of a camp-fire, and I knew that I had been surprised by a band of Indians who were preparing to hold some rite of their old religion. Though I had not been invited to their ceremony, neither had I invited them to intrude upon my contemplation, so I remained and watched them. (Yes, there is less secrecy out here, for the reason that there is greater understanding and greater tolerance.) Soon I was looking on at a strange dance. All in a circle they swung round and round the blazing fire, singing and leaping. I did not know the meaning of the words they sang; but I could read their minds by the thought-images they formed, and I knew that they were celebrating the date—reached by what lunar reckoning I knew not—of some great Indian massacre in which they had taken part a hundred or two hundred years ago.

And the impulse of their dance, the motive power of it, was hatred of the white man who had scattered them and driven them away from their old hunting grounds. Shocked, yet fascinated by this inner glimpse at the souls of the American aborigines, I watched them. Though I am not skilled in magic rituals, I soon perceived that there was form and method in this dance, method and form and a hostile purpose. They were, by exciting themselves and by fixity of thought, trying to excite a scattered company of men in these United States—men of a low grade of intellect but of psychic temperament—to deeds of violence and destruction.

"So that is the way they do it!" I thought. Then I drew a veil around my thoughts, that they might not be perceived by the beings before me. Yes, I can do that, and so can many men upon the earth. I could smell the keen fresh odors of the pine grove, and I could feel the rising wind as it swept across the clearing; for the wind seemed to respond to their call and to offer its forces to them. You must know that the elements are impersonal, though semi-personalities inhabit them, and that the elements *and* these semi-personalities can be used and guided, for purposes good or evil, by any being who has gained that peculiar power in one or many lives.

And looking off in the distance, I could see that the wind as it swept along carried the thoughts and passions of these long dead men, these souls that by reason of their own downward tendencies had not broken away from the attraction of matter, the astral gravitation that makes so many souls earthbound. Still looking off and projecting my consciousness in a way I have learned to do, I saw the influence of this magic ritual of revenge and menace as it touched the minds of men far scattered. I saw their thoughts take on suddenly the tinge of hatred, hatred for the civilization in which they had failed to realize their personal desires. And I knew that on that night and on the morrow, and at intervals for many days, deeds of violence would be committed, that property would be destroyed, and men of order threatened.

My heart was sad, for I had not understood before how real was the danger to my country in these times of crisis from the karma the old settlers had made. Of course they believed they were doing right in ridding themselves and their adopted land from the simple but complex natives, whose civilization was older than the civilization of Europe, and who had loved this land as only those can love a land who have known the freedom of its spaces. When the magic dance was over, and one by one and two by two the communicants slipped away among the shadows, I strode forward into the circle to have speech with any who should willingly respond to my desire for acquaintanceship. Suddenly I found myself face to face with a majestic chieftain, wearing one of those long feather bonnets whose every feather marks some deed of daring or achievement. (What a splendid custom was that! What an incentive to action! Truly among the red men, deed won a feather in the cap.)

His face was like that of a hawk, and his eyes were bright with an inner fire, that intensity of feeling and thought commingled which marks the leader and master of men and him alone. And I said to him in the forms of thought, for I knew no word of his old language: "I have been an unintentional witness to your ceremony this evening. Will you enlighten me further as to its purpose? For I see that it was directed towards the land of breathing men." With a sweep of his authoritative arm he dismissed the few of his companions who had not already moved away among the trees, and we two were alone together. "I come as a friend," I said, seeing that he hesitated.

And the word was true; for I saw that whatever harm he mistakenly sought to accomplish, in his soul was the consciousness of justice, that fundamental balance between right and wrong, that proposition of law, which when native in the mind gives it dignity and attracts respect. This was no dabbler in aboriginal and nasty sorcery, but a kind of priest of retribution, a tribal demigod who might perhaps some day be made constructive and not destructive, an instrument of the great Genius of America of which I have spoken in a former letter, the Weaver of Destiny who has our land in charge. We measured each other with the eyes, and I cast aside the veil that I had before drawn around my thoughts, that he might see me mind to mind and realize that I respected and to a degree understood him.

"You have seen what you have seen," he observed. "And you do not resent my presence?" "No." The fresh odor of the pine grove was keen in my senses, and my newfound companion threw back his head with a splendid motion as if to drink it in. "Freedom is good," he said, "and the land was ours." So I perceived that by excusing himself and his associates he had perceived that I accused them. Then I knew that I could really commune with him mind to mind, and I was glad; for I ever seek to extend the range of my knowledge and to form acquaintance with those of sturdy will. "But the land is free to all the world," I said, "to you and to me, and to those of both our races."

"We do not see it so," was his reply. "But," I insisted, "are we not now, you and I, enjoying it in freedom?" It is difficult to translate in words the rapid give and take of our thoughts, the pictures that flashed back and forth between us, as I strove with kindliness and will to make him understand that the welfare of his race did not call for the destruction of mine. I told him—and the idea was so new to him that, lacking words, I had to draw my story on the canvas of thought in the minutest detail—how the soul that leaves the earth for a time returns to it in another form. And I explained how hundreds upon hundreds of his people, and the most advanced among them, had already come back in material form to that America they had loved before, that they wore white bodies, and could only be distinguished from other white men by the keenness of their eyes, their gait, and certain peculiarities of speech and manner.

He followed my story with astonished, almost painful, intensity; for he knew, with that inner knowledge which on this side of life is almost impossible to deceive, that I spoke honestly and believed that which I told him. "And do you not deceive yourself?" was his inevitable question. Then I told him of those recent and former lives of my own which I most vividly remember, and cited proofs that I did not deceive myself. "But what a life is that of the white man for one of my people?" he demanded.

Then he flashed me picture after picture of the simple white man's life in America, the schoolhouse with the choking hot stove and the bad air, the house and home

71

with closed doors and windows, the "meeting house" where a droning or a noisy preacher prated of things he did not understand, to others who believe or did not believe that they believed him. He held up before me as for ridicule the clothing of the white man in the lower walks of life, the confining and uncomfortable shoes, the binding trousers, the ugly hat that makes bald the head, and the collar. The one he pictured was a paper collar, soiled and wilted at the edges. Then he showed me—as if to prove the breadth of his observations—an office in a city, with the clerks seated upon stools and bent with aching backs over ledgers that contained figures, figures, long lines of figures that were the symbols of the white man's wampum, which seemed so trivial when made the principal occupation of a soul that had rejoiced in the red man's forest.

"And is it for this that they come back to their native land?" he asked. "But the soul must gain all experience," I said. The idea seemed new to him, and he pondered it with knitted brows. "Why should the soul gain all experience?" he asked. "That it may return to its God rich in knowledge," I replied. "Its God." At that thought the strange eyes of him lighted, though his face remained immobile. "Yes," I said, "for your God and my God are both God." "There are many gods," he replied. "There is the Great Spirit, and there are the others."

"In the center of each of them," I assured him, "there is a spot, a core of the heart that is the same in all, that exists everywhere, and in every heart is one, that knows no division; and that center is also in your heart and mine and in that of our respective Gods." "Did you learn that in one of those hot schoolhouses?" he asked. "No. I did not learn it even when I was an old man upon the earth, but after I came out here. On earth I rather prided myself on my separateness." "Then one can learn new religions out here?" he asked, in surprise. "If one finds a teacher," I replied. "But what need is there of *new* religions?"

"There is," I said, "in the core of every religion also that central spot where all are one. And there is in all races," I pursued, for I saw that he watched with half-belief, "there is in all races a core of unity. The red man is the brother and not the permanent enemy of the white man. So why should you injure the descendants of those who followed what they believed to be right in extending their holdings in this land long ago?" "But I was not seeking to injure them for injury's sake." "Then I misunderstood the purpose of your magic song." "Oh!" he exclaimed. "You caught the feeling of my children, who cannot see beyond feeling. My purpose is only to destroy the present to make way for the old life."

"But the present is always a stage," I said, "on the highroad that leads to the future. And my people reincarnated, and yours reincarnated—or so many of them as are ready to go on—shall go on together and in this land. They will form, with those who join them from beyond the seas, a new race. And thanks to the labors of a few among the white men who have studied and appreciated the traditions and civilization of the red man and sought to save them from utter obliteration, the old forest lore will become a part of the inheritance of that new race which is to grow out of the union of yours and mine and the others. And for a part of every year, when the life of the new race is adjusted, the boys and girls and men and women will go out to the wilds and enjoy the freedom of the tent and the society round the campfire, and we shall be brothers—real blood brothers—at last, and all the old wounds shall be healed. Can you not recognize me as your brother?" He nodded his head.

"And will you not spread among your people the glad tidings of the new race, in all of whose possessions they will share?" We stood long looking in each other's eyes, and I told him more than I could record here if I held the use of your pencil for many hours. In the end he understood me. It is my belief that he will spread the story among his people, and that one danger will be lessened thereby, to some degree, for the children of the new race.

The Ideal of Success

June 23, 1917

PUT FEAR OUT OF your hearts. The future will give you no greater lessons than you can master. It is not well to know the future in complete detail. Had the world known during the last ten years all it would be obliged to suffer in this war, would it have made the progress it has made in art, science and commerce? No. Every thought would have been haunted. You may say that the weaker races (and the stronger ones) would have made better preparation. But a part of this lesson has been not to delay inevitable preparation, and to know in future that a nation which idealizes war and is mostly army, has not cultivated that ideal and that army solely for its own amusement.

If you want to understand national life and individual life, you must look for their dominating ideals. An ideal is a tendency. What is the dominating ideal of America? Summed in a word, it is success, is it not? Now America is in a great war, and you may be sure that she will leave nothing undone that can make for success in that war, as she has left nothing undone that could make for success in business. Take your own case. What are your dominating ideals and tendencies? You would say, offhand, work and study and intellectual companionship, would you not? Very well. As to work, do not fear a future in which good work is pretty sure of at least a living wage.

Study? There will always be books to feed your hunger for reading. Companionship? There are too many lonely souls in the world for you ever to be lonely.

What else? You lift your pencil and think. That is about all, is it not? Now let us return to America. America is not—has not been—a warlike nation, except when threatened by injustice, to herself or others. Will she lose this war? I think not. But there will be complexities regarding the end of this war. I want to refer to something I said in a recent letter, that we were organizing on this side of the airy frontier for work for the future of America. I have spoken of the Genius of this land, a composite entity you may call it, if your imagination is not equal to the task of seeing that you—all of you—are cells in the body of the Genius of America.

Now the Genius of this land has glorious purposes, and she uses you—all of you—for her purposes, as you use the cells of your body, as you are using at this moment the aggregation of cells that form the hand with which you hold your pencil. In registering yourselves at the call of your country, you are affirming your acceptance of the office of cells in the great body of her. Some of you she must sacrifice in the war for the welfare of the whole, as every day cells die and are born in the body of man, the microcosm. Extend the idea to the whole human race, and the figure will be still more apt. The genius of the race is suffering now. The process will ultimate in a more perfect health.

You perhaps protest that many of those who are dying are the flower of the race, the young, the fitted to survive. But do you not remember that their souls survive? The essential part of them is not lost, but set free for a greater work. Have you considered that earth-life may be the dream, and the life after death the waking? Sages have considered it before you, and accepted the possibility. Out here we are hopeful, and very busy. It is because I am so busy that I come to you only occasionally. Do not hurry me, for I do not hurry you. We have problems to solve out here. As I have said, one of our problems is the great number of Indian souls, red men souls, who went out of life with resentment and revenge in their hearts for the elimination of their race by the white man in America.

Somehow we must placate them, and enlist them on your side. Otherwise they may be a dangerous element for the future. Some of them would like to see your civilization destroyed, as theirs was destroyed, and a few of them are strong enough to do real harm. The best way to make an enemy harmless is to understand his peculiar qualities, to learn something from the frankness of his enmity, to turn away evil by letting it go off at a tangent. But the Indian souls are not famous for their frankness. Even with me they sometimes conceal their resentment—deep, fundamental—at the "theft," as they feel it, of the land where they once roamed in freedom. I advise America to cultivate the free life of the open. I have advised you in a former book that the old woodcraft should be resuscitated and taught to the children. There may come a time when the rudiments of this knowledge will be useful to many of you.

Great changes are coming in the world, a period of adjustment to new conditions. There is a restless element in all adjustment, and national restlessness is like that of puberty; it needs to be minimized by healthful outdoor play, or by work which masquerades as play. The future will take from the present those elements that are most important for survival. Do not fear that we shall return to the Dark Ages. Oh, no. We are going into a Light Age. It is only twilight now.

LETTER 18

Order and Progress

July 18, 1917

OUR PURPOSE IS TO make the changes that must come, come gradually. We want to avoid sudden changes. You in the world have no faint idea of the influence and power we can wield on our side. We can speak to the minds of men without their knowing whence the ideas come. They think, when a sudden idea comes into their minds, that they have evolved it; but *sudden* ideas generally come from outside. (I put one in your mind this morning, then ran away before you could recognize me. Why did I run away? Because I wanted you to use your own judgment.)

Just at present we are trying to encourage America as to her future—*her orderly and peaceful future*, after peace is declared in Europe. You may as well know that there are many out here who are anxious about the future of the world. All men do not cease to worry when they have left their bodies. There are many here who think the world is going to smash. They always had that fear in life whenever things seemed to go wrong; and now they are no less inclined to accept every complexity as an omen of failure and confusion.

All over America there are men and women—and many of them are in pulpits or on platforms—who are croaking away about the destruction of society following this war. Bless your troubled hearts! Society is not going to be destroyed. Some elements in society will be gradually done away with, and good riddance to them! But society has made too great advance, in mechanical and intellectual ways, to permit its structure to be pulled from beneath its feet. Do not worry. Watch out, but do not worry. As Abraham Lincoln once prevented this country from being territorially divided and thus weakened, so he and others are now working to prevent a spiritual division that would be even more disastrous. No, we are not going to see your useful inventions and your structures that the future has need of, cast into the rubbish heap by reckless violence and extravagance. What is useful must be conserved. What is useless for the future can be made over into something useful.

Humanity has not been in the habit of taking sudden jumps. It has put one foot regularly before the other, and gone ahead rather steadily. The way of man in the past has been to improve and make over, rather than suddenly to discard its institutions, or even its garments. Only that which is really worn out is cast away. And our financial system, and our social system in general, will be improved and *not discarded*. Did you think we were going back to wampum? Oh, no! There *is* a strong pull from this side, and from those who inhabited your continent, to simplify the life in America. But America is no longer isolated. She has now taken her place in the republic of nations.

Some of the souls who used to be American Indians would like to see America resume wigwams and campfires, because those souls want to come back, and they dread the complexity of modern American life. But there are teachers here—and some of them red teachers—who can instruct the souls behindhand in adaptability. I have told you that there is an influence tending to draw America backward. But I have not told you to be panicky regarding the fact. There are reactionaries—even in your world. The influence from this side is subtle. But the majority here who desire to lead the world, desire to lead it forward and not back. *The world will go forward.*

Yes, the souls you call the "departed" are organizing themselves. They realize that their influence can be more effective if it has a purpose and a program. For a time after the war began there was great confusion out here, but things are becoming more orderly. Minds are becoming more united. Many of us who have common sense and some measure of political judgment give most of our time to lecturing here and there, wherever we can draw a crowd together. That is one reason why you have seen me so seldom of late. I have been busier than ever before. Knowing that a time is coming soon when I can rest from my present labors, I am using my strength as fast as I generate it. For those whom I convince that America and other countries are going forward—*must* go forward to greater activity—seek to convince others in their turn. No lecturer on earth ever had so busy a month as I have had this last month. I have spoken to hundreds several times every day, going from place to place, from State to State, from city to city. I can speak in San Francisco in the morning, in New York at noon, in New Orleans at two o'clock, in Butte, Montana, in the evening. I am not limited to railway timetables, nor do I pay my fare.

Believe me, we are going to save America, and we are going to save the world. For the Masters are behind us, and they will not let the world be destroyed. I should not like you to know how near it has been to destruction more than once during the last three years. But the forces of premeditated evil against which we fought so long have been scattered now, and though they have not been destroyed, their effect has been greatly lessened. What we have reason to fear now is the unwisdom of those who believe they wish good to the world—*the unwisdom of fanatics and agitators and fuss budgets* of all sorts, stirring up confusion and darkening counsel with their unpractical and conflicting ideas.

Order, order, order! That is what the world must strive for in the period of reaction which will follow this war. The reaction must be reckoned with; but it will be only a brief rest of over wearied hearts, who will again begin building. It is in that building period that I hope for America, because she will be less tired than the other members of the great world brotherhood. But in America at that time there will be a danger. I tell you that, lest you be taken unawares and relax your attention. Be watchful, but not over-anxious. And trust the Masters of Life somehow to lead you through.

LETTER 19

The Federation of Nations

August 9, 1917

T HE TIME HAS COME now for America to get out into the world and take her place in the federation of nations. Let her unite with England in a strong bond, and thereby she can keep the peace of the world. The isolation of America in the past has been in line with her destiny; it was necessary for her to develop to her present state of power without interruptions, or the influence of international complications upon her statesmen. Free and alone, she has not had to become a part of the great and creaking machine of international diplomacy and intrigue. But now she is independent, and, politically speaking, her character is formed. You may say that America has attained her majority, and is entitled to vote in the councils and elections of the world.

She has much to do for both France and England, as they have both done so much for her in the past. They have formed her culture and influenced her spirit; now she will influence their spirit. When you read the other day of the work which our soldiers are doing in France, helping in many little ways in the villages and on the farms, your heart glowed with pleasure; you remembered what I said to you before America came into the war, that our men were to go to France and to work, work, work for the rebuilding of France.

That is only the beginning. More and more will our men work over there, during and after war. Soon there will come a call for a new kind of work—new for us. There is deep meaning in this bringing together of the nations for a common cause. From that, there is only a step to the bringing together of *all* nations for *one* cause. The force of revolt in the world must spend itself, as the force of race hatred has spent itself—for it is already spent. The continuation of the war will be practically without the rage of the beginning. We go on because it is our job, and even in New York now there is no longer the fierceness of two years ago. And in England it has lessened, and in France it is lessened, and in Germany it is lessened. War has now become a task like any other, to be gone through with. When it no longer seems worthwhile, it will stop.

The question of America's part in the federation of states interests me now.

The New Ideal

August 19, 1917

S INCE GERMANY EVOLVED her idea of flamboyant nationalism and tried to foist it upon the world in imperial fashion, the world has grown skeptical of the national fetish. It will believe in the good intentions of no nation or race that flaunts its perfections in the face of friend or enemy. America, as she grows more and more sure of her high destiny, must also grow more modest. She must realize herself as one of the sister states in the great commonwealth of nations, and the eagle will take lessons in voice culture. As a quiet voice can make itself heard in a medley of noises where a screaming voice would be inaudible, so must America's voice become deep and quiet.

She is paying for her place in the councils of the world. Let her voice be heard by reason of its dignified and restrained accents. A great change is taking place in Europe, in its conception of the American character. Hitherto France has known the American tourist, and the uprooted American who lived there in preference to his own country. Now France is learning something about the American man in his work a day, play a day, fighting and loving, living and dying sublimity. She has rubbed her eyes as she watched him, wondering if she were awake. She has recognized a new type. She does not understand it yet, but she wants to understand it.

There is a new and disturbing warmth now at the heart of France for this new brother from across the seas. She sees (for she is subtle) the crudity of him as measured by her more artificial standards. But she sees also the grandeur and chivalry of him, as compared with her old idea of the foreigner.

Ah, America and Americans! You are on trial now in the courts of the world's judgment as you have never been before. My heart is aglow as I see our boys go out into the larger world, carrying with them the clear outdoor spirit of the American plains and woodlands. When I see the eyes of the sublime and pain-chastened French grow deep and warm as they rest upon our boys, I am so proud of them! I forget that I am also uprooted, having left the land of my birth for the regions beyond death.

In the councils at the ending of the war and after the war, may the modesty of greatness restrain America from any suggestion to France or England that she saved them from destruction. I clasp my hands—to you they would be shadowy hands—together with excess of emotion, as I pray for the guidance of America in the councils that are to come. Modesty—let that be the watchword. The soul of France is aflame with gratitude, the soul of France is aflame with love. The hearts of the French people in the night grow warm and their eyes grow wet as they whisper to themselves, *"Les Américains! Les Américains!"* Oh, be mindful of the love you have won! I would die all over again a thousand times rather than see my Americans disappoint their French brethren in this crisis of the world's life.

You wonder why I say nothing of England? Ah!

England knows you already. England has known you long. You cannot surprise England. She knows you as the mother knows her son or daughter; but to the French you are a mystery, a mystery that has come to help, an angel in a khaki shirt and a slouch hat and a strange voice. Don't you understand? She prays for you. She would pray *to* you if she were not so shy in her love. There is a new strange wonder in her eyes, and a sweet thrill all over her. Oh, exalt the brotherhood of nations—that never before realized ideal! You cannot take away from a boy who has grown up in a free world the deep-rooted idea that America is and ever must be free. In years gone by the sons of this soil have died for freedom, freedom for themselves, freedom for the black man. Now they fight and die for the freedom of the world.

Do you know what it means to be free? Only the self-restrained man is free, for lawlessness is not freedom. Lawlessness is always in leash to passions tyrannical. In the new America that I see just over the edge of the horizon (for my eye reaches farther than yours), there will be room for the fullest development of the individual idea, while the idea of social responsibility will make it stable. Hitherto individuality has run rampant. Witness the hoarding of food by a few, while many go without. Watch the clash and struggle of each interest to take some advantage for itself out of this tragic opportunity. Before the war is ended the hearts of men must work in harness with their minds. The old generation is dying off, the generation whose initiation girdled the continent with railroads, spurred by the hope of personal gain. The new men who will follow the old "captains of industry" will glimpse a new ideal. I am told by one who knows more than I that the men who have made industrial America, by their foresight and initiative, were guided and inspired by Beings who used them and their ambitions for world purposes beyond their comprehension.

LETTER 21

A Rambling Talk

November 15, 1917

I AM NOT IN A literary mood tonight, so I may talk in a rambling way. I wonder if you know the seriousness of the enterprise which America has undertaken. You think you do. But before the matter is all threshed out at the end you may have surprises in store.

Do not worry about your things in London. London is large, and a good many bombs can fall without destroying any great portion of it. Yes, I say emphatically again what I said some two years and a half ago, that there will be internal troubles in Germany—and in other places, too. The world is going to be made over. Do not be afraid. The making over of the world will not hurt you.

Humanity is so afraid of change! The race has gone through many changes—some of them in prehistoric times—more dramatic than the present change. Humanity has a long history, and little of it is recorded in books that you can read. Yes, the world will be united, and the world will be cut up. That sounds like a paradox, perhaps. As I am resting tonight, I may take the liberty of being disconnected. You ought always to live in a quiet place like this, a little remote from the center of things. You do not belong in the bustle and crowd downtown, either in New York or any other large city. All those who have developed their inner senses should live a little apart. That does not mean that they should all become hermits; but they should live in the outskirts. When you feel a desire for the crowd you can go down into it.

Tell—not to worry because this book is going slowly. You are not working against time. The world will go on, and you will go with it. Make no mistake about that. The world is going very fast. All these new "Psychic" books are evidence that the world is going fast. A few years ago no publisher would have issued them. I do not wonder that your head swims a little.

You have been impressed by "losing" so many personal friends since the war began, friends whose deaths seemed unconnected with the war. But they are of those who could not adjust to the new world that is coming. Their Silent Watchers are taking them out. You each have a Silent Watcher, a something, a part of you that is above and beyond you, yet which is the most real of all the parts of you. The Watchers of the universe are watching more intently than usual. Your own is watching you as well as the world. It will give you notice when any important action is necessary. It seems as if the world had adjusted itself to the idea that the dead *may* speak with the living. But that is only the beginning of knowledge.

When the worst of the war is over, and men begin to adapt themselves to peace, they will try to know themselves. And they will discover that their bodies and souls are only parts of them, that they exist on as many planes of being as there are planes of matter and of subtler substance, and that each of these selves is as real as the personality they see in the mirror. They will learn to form links between them, to build bridges of communication. Finally they will become consciously complete beings.

Joy is coming back to the world some day, such joy as the world has never known. You will one day be glad to be alive again, and I mean all of you. Do not fret because you have to remain in America. At the moment America is a good place in which to be. The world is opening its eyes at the efficiency of America. She is setting an example that her friends will be ashamed not to follow. Some day she will set the highest example of all.

The Lever of World Unity

November 19, 1917

DO YOU NOT SEE that the unifying influence of America is already being felt in the war? Do you not see how America, through the President of the United States, is drawing the Allies together? That is her destiny, to assemble all nations in a brotherhood of democratic freedom and mutual helpfulness. This demand of President Wilson for a council, for unified action in prosecuting the war, is one of the most significant events in history. For the first time a group of friendly nations may really work as one, putting aside all personal jealousies and fears—for a great world end.

It is the lever of world unity which shall lift the burden of wastefulness that heretofore has cost the world half the fruits of its labor. Oh, nations of Europe; do not fear the great free land across the waters! She wants nothing of you, save now the privilege of helping you to save yourselves, and in the future to work with you for the ideals that will make you all strong. The Anglo-Saxon race must again be like one family, though in two houses; but bye and bye, when America shall have amalgamated her foreign residents with herself in one indissoluble race, she will still be your sister, O Britain! And you two shall counsel together for the further enlightening of the world.

Sometimes I go high in the etheric regions and look

down upon the earth, so high that the horizons bound one hemisphere after another. The horizons of time are also thus expanded, and I see ahead of and behind the present hour. I see the causes that have brought the world to its present *impasse.* You will have to remove the wall that separates you from the age of enlightened brotherhood. You have read about the golden age of the past. Did you think it was a fanciful story, to amuse children in the firelight? I tell you it will sometime be realized again, and on this earth—now rent by hatred and war.

You must retain all you have won from the mines of the earth and from the activity of your own brains. Inventions and arts, they will all have their place in the new age that is coming, and hitherto unimagined art and science will add further to the glory and comfort of life. It will be the fault of your own folly and blindness if you lose anything of value to the soul. The soul needs matter as matter needs the soul. Because we look forward to an age without hatred and wasteful division, we do not look forward to an age of idleness and inertia. Limitless will be the opportunities for genius, for talent, for ambition. The greatest aristocracy of earth is the aristocracy of mind and soul, and mind and soul will be cultivated. The education of the future will be not only practical but humanistic; nothing will be thrown away that makes for beauty or for thought. The treasures of dead languages will not be thrown into the dustbin. After the labor necessary to provide for the material wants of the world, time will be left for art and beauty and scholarship, for social discussion and religious exaltation. The mystic also will have his place.

Three years ago I would not have dared to prophesy

a *happy* outcome for this tragic fracas. More than two years ago I told you that the battle had been won in the regions above the earth—won by the powers of good, who labor for the welfare of mankind. How *can* you doubt? If the war had ended two years ago, the world might have gone on more or less as it went before. But now it can never go back to the old selfish ways. In the need that will follow the war the races will help one another; they will turn to one another as brothers and sisters turn. Never lose faith that out of this tragedy will come the guerdon of the world's desire. I see it, I live for it (for I live more vitally than you); and that you may see and live for it also I struggle against the lightness of my present body, that has a tendency to carry me away from the dense regions where you suffer and pray, you men of earth.

You who have followed me from those early days when I wrote you letters from the lower astral world, describing as a traveler in a strange country the things I had seen; you who followed me through the hells of astral turmoil during the early months of the war, follow me yet a little further. I will show you the way as it has been shown to me. And you will walk in that way, though stumbling at first and groping for the thread of purpose through the labyrinth of reconstruction, in the days that shall be called days of peace. For perfect peace will not come at once. You will have to work for it, as you have worked for triumph in war. But if you have faith, you will ride the stormy waters into the haven of a new earth. And a new heaven will spread above the earth, for heaven is largely peopled from below; it recruits its population from below. No new angels are being created now. The outgoing Breath rests, and the drawing in of Breath is about to begin. You who have practiced "yogi breathing" know how difficult it is to hold the breath *out* for more than a short time. It can only be done by force of will. The tendency is to return, as the tendency in the race is to return towards the Source from which it came. It is therefore I say that you cannot retard, save for a little while, the flow of the race-breath towards harmony and peace and love.

The struggle of men with each other in the selfishness of separation is like the struggle of the yogi not to in-breathe—the young and inexperienced yogi; for the wise one breathes at stated intervals, and knows when the period is full. The race knows. It will follow the law of the outflow and inflow. You cannot prevent it. So yield yourselves to the current that would carry you back to God. It will not be a hurried journey, for the in-flowing breath is measured too. There will be time for labor and for rest, and to gather flowers by the way. Do you fear the return to God, however slow it may be? I who have tasted death know there is nothing to fear; and I who have tasted the new life tell you there is everything to hope.

LETTER 23

The Stars of Man's Destiny

November 24, 1917

HAS IT OCCURRED TO you that the powers that have in charge the progress of the world may be obliged to use methods repugnant to your desires, in order to accomplish inevitable purposes at the time when they are due? Man, by rebelling against the tendencies of cosmic progress, may retard it—for a time; but when the wave rises high enough it will carry him along against his will, and inevitable effects are produced in spite of his rebellion.

Take this war. The hour had struck on the world clock when races of men should work together for a common purpose. They rebelled in their fear that each would not get his share of world benefits; so the world was attacked by a common enemy, and the races have *had* to unite for a common purpose, that of preserving civilization from the destruction that threatens it. Could this war have been prevented? By prevision, yes. But no one with influence enough to be heard respectfully had that prevision. Those who stand high in the world's regard have generally so concentrated upon their individual work and their individual ambitions, that they have lost the ability to see impersonally and to see the world as a whole. Some can see as a whole the tendencies of their own country; few can see the world tendency.

And I tell you now that if, when this universal war is

ended, the races do not recognize the necessity to unite in a federation for the good of all, there will be after forty years little left of all that has been accomplished during that marvelous nineteenth century which saw material progress equaling that of the preceding two thousand years. Can man not see the stars of his destiny without being struck on the head with a hammer? If man will not work for the good of the whole, then the whole has to be threatened. It is so threatened now, if you could see it.

LETTER 24

Melancholy

December 23, 1917

I WANT TO WRITE ABOUT melancholy, not the depression produced by bad digestion or pressure on the nerves, but that cloud of darkness that sometimes descends upon the most brilliant mind and the stoutest heart, making them for a while useless for any purpose—except that of drawing knowledge from the experience of melancholy itself.

Not all sadness originates in the heart that is sad, and fear, the basis of melancholy, may be suggested to a soul on earth by a soul beyond the earth. You do not realize what a cloud of dissatisfied and fearful souls this holocaust has let loose on the invisible regions; they flock round the sensitive souls upon the earth, longing to "tell their troubles," longing for sympathy and help. They are no more self-reliant than many in your world whose very presence depresses a stronger fellow being. Now whenever you feel that cloud of melancholy, stop and ascertain the cause. You have observed the workings of suggestion. If you find nothing in your environment or circumstances to fill you with hopelessness, would it not be safe to assume—unless you are bilious—that the cloud gathered elsewhere and merely descended upon you? The student who hopes someday—though maybe many lives in the future—to achieve adeptship, may as well begin now to control and direct his thoughts and feelings.

You need not be melancholy unless you want to be. There are texts, mantras, adages, even copybook maxims you can recall and meditate upon, that will drive away the worst fit of the blues. Here are a few: Pleasure and pain are opposite expressions of one force. I am a part of God, and no harm can overtake God. What is the truth hidden in this well of discontent? If I go deep enough into this midnight earth, I shall come out on the other side where the sun shines. I was happy yesterday, and I am still I. A frightened dog will never scare away a robber. If all these ills befall me, it will be an exercise of power to conquer them. Not very profound, perhaps; but you can write better ones if you wish. I am merely illustrating one process of shaking off the burden of dread.

Why should you men dread anything? Even death is only dreadful when you are afraid of it. The Masters enjoy difficulties. They are the acid that tests the gold of their mastership. And speaking from a lower plane, there is pleasure in doing any difficult thing. Why, in the writing of a big novel there is more actual work, mental and physical, than in overcoming some great misfortune. It is less work to go out and overcome a threatened misfortune than it is to write a short story.

How anybody in good health and with even ordinary ability can yield to melancholy is a question for a philosopher. I am not talking now of grief for dead friends, or for false friends, which grief is far worse; but of the fear of some imaginary disaster which in all probability will never happen. The surest way to attract disasters is to imagine them. You can create almost anything if you imagine it strongly enough—even joy and courage. A Master once told me that the control and exorcism of melancholy was a greater test of power than the control of desire.

Both often come from outside, are suggested to the receptive, passive mind. Now the Master entertains only those suggestions that can strengthen his purposes. If you have a friend that makes you courageous by his very presence, cultivate his society. If you have a friend who makes you melancholy, either teach him better or get rid of him; send him to a doctor. What is the use in our talking about occult power if we have not power over our moods? Practice on moods. As an exercise, some time when you are active, force yourself to be lazy. When you are lazy and not tired, force yourself to be active. Natural fatigue should not be pressed too far, it is a mere reaction; but indolence is not fatigue. It is in the physical what melancholy is in the mental. As another exercise, when your mind circles round and round something, switch it off as you would switch off an electric light. Turn and think of something else. You can do it.

And, by the way, one of the best cures for melancholy is an hour of mathematical calculations. I defy anybody to be melancholy in the arms of geometry or trigonometry. Why? You cannot think in mathematical terms and of yourself at the same time. People always think of themselves when they are melancholy. But you tell me that you became melancholy the other day in thinking about a friend who had lost her job. Think again. By wondering what you could do for this friend and whether you could afford it, you began to fear. Is it not so? You may be sad because a friend is in trouble, but you cannot be melancholy for anyone but yourself. Another can make you melancholy by making you morbid and fearful.

Our thoughts are so chained to our ego that it is difficult for them to escape for long. But are you ever melancholy when creating imaginatively a scene in a book? Could you be melancholy when figuring the "polar elevation" of a planet, or computing one of those converse "primary directions"? I see you smile. When you are engaged with figures you forget yourself. Now take my advice. When auto-suggestion is powerless to conquer melancholy, draw up an astrological figure in a low attitude with that table of oblique ascensions that I saw you using yesterday, and work out the converse primaries and the longitude of Vulcan. You remind me that when on earth I had small interest in astrology. But I am talking about mathematical calculations.

LETTER 25

Compensatory Play

February 1, 1918

I HAVE LOOKED IN ON you occasionally during the last few weeks, pleased with your resting for a time. The ambitious and energetic are prone to underestimate the value of occasional idleness. You cannot run even a machine all the time without oil and rest. Neither can the most vigorous engineer-soul run its brain and body too long without letting them cool. The farmer knows when to let a field lie fallow. "After the war" it is to be hoped that the soldiers who have worked so long at one labor—that of war—may be given a period of compensatory play, doing nothing, before being replaced in the hive of industry. Let them enjoy the breezes and the perfume of idleness for a little time; the reaction from that rest will send them back into the workshops with renewed desire for activity. If the world has to get along with less for a few weeks, that will not hurt the world.

In the years to come there will be more rest and recreation in America. In Europe there is going to be some degree of fatigue after this war, and America can easily hold her own if she carries a lower steam pressure. The idle hours are sometimes as valuable as those that are spent in labor. It is in so-called idle hours that we meditate, get acquainted with ourselves, build air castles, which are working plans for our edifice of the future. Day dreams are good. I had a day dream during my

102

life, and it was really the working-plan for the future I am building now. I wanted to get back something I had lost, and I have got it back. You wonder what it was? I do not mind telling you. In a former life I went far along the road towards mastership. Then once upon a time I slipped back a long way. My day dream was to recover that lost ground, and I have recovered much of it out here.

If I had not left the world with that day dream vivid in my consciousness, I should not have made the progress and the recovery I have made. I was talking the other day with an old friend—a very dear old friend—who came out here a year or two ago, and she and I agreed that the day dreams we had dreamed together were among the most valuable products of our recent life. She is reveling in the recovery of her own lost ground, and she will run me a good race as the years go on. Yes, one can race across recovered ground of adeptship.

My friend said laughingly the other day that she had made more plans since coming out here than she could execute in a long while. "Take your time," I advised, "in the execution. You have all eternity." She looked at me in the old way I remember so well, and said: "Time may be made for slaves, but eternity is made for masters." She too is glad that she came out. She had done one kind of work long enough, and is now enjoying another. Is she helping me, you wonder? Well, no, unless you count the pleasure of our renewed association as help. Why should she help me, or I her? Our work is our own.

You in the world should help each other when you can; but out here we of equal stature help each other by *being*. That is a good help, though, the being together sometimes. What a wonderful expression, by the way, "being together"! What poetry! Not working together, nor playing together, but simply being. You must often have felt that joy when with a loved friend. Words are not necessary for that enjoyment. Words often lessen that enjoyment by the very effort of uttering them. Effortless being! Even the birds enjoy it, and the rose could give you valuable secrets of that joy.

In the world I have heard busy bodies say of a beautiful woman that she did nothing. What of it? A rose does not run a sewing machine, or write books. Joy is coming back to the world. It has been long absent. Being for its own sake has taken on new meanings in the minds of those who are glad to be still alive. To have passed through all the perils of a long war and still to "be" a living man is something to make the soul wonder. The men who have fought in this war from the beginning should not be crowded too hard when at last they can stretch their limbs in the hammocks of peace. They have earned the right. As they spin their soldier yarns, gaze at them with respect. They passed through the shadow of death for you. That God has retained them among the active cells of His body is because He has need of them still; but it does not mean that they should go on working for you every minute. Suppose you work for them for a while. When they are rested they will join you in your labor.

Last night I listened to two soldiers talking, and this is what they said to each other: "What will you do, John, when it's all over?" "I'll lie in the bath tub an hour every morning, in the warm, soft, soapy water; and in the afternoon I'll call on one dear girl after another, and drink tea, and listen to their talk. And what will you do?" "Oh, I'll just look at my wife and hold her hand." Idle talk, you think? That depends upon what you mean by idle talk. To me that talk was immensely significant. Soon after our little skirmish with Spain I remember hearing an active woman say of her husband that he had never been good for anything since he came back from Cuba. "Well," I said, "he was good for a lot in Cuba." The Spanish-American war! A fly beside an elephant, as compared with this war. And the German is tired, too. You may not have to overwork yourself to keep up with him after the war.

LETTER 26

The Aquarian Age

February 2, 1918

YOU HAVE WONDERED why the Masters speak now of the interests of the common man, while in former times they said little about them. But do you not know that when the need for a thing has come, the work of the Masters with the world is to urge the world in the direction of its destiny? You have read of the iron age, the golden age, etc., and that the golden age follows the iron. You may have wondered how states so utterly dissimilar could be juxtaposed. Now between the iron age and the golden age there is a period of transition, a period short as compared with one of the great ages, for example the longest one, the golden, which is given as one million, seven hundred and twenty-eight thousand years.

I have not visited you this evening to announce that the golden age is immediately at hand. Oh, no! But we approach the termination of a minor cycle, and the period of transition from the present state of the world to the next will be of about one thousand years. That is to say, this period of one thousand years will bring us to the middle of what is called the Aquarian Age, for the half of one of these lesser Zodiacal periods is approximately of that length.

What is the Aquarian Age? You know the humanitarian nature of Aquarius. You also know the characteristics of the planet Uranus, to which Aquarius is now attributed. Well, the inference is obvious. We shall have an Aquarian world, and a world where things will go after the manner of that strange and abrupt planet Uranus. The old fashioned world is passing away, the Jupiterian world, and we are entering upon a period of change, political, social, religious and personal. There is going to be an attempt at a federation of states, a federation of souls. Nothing but this war could have effected it—with the suddenness characteristic of that mysterious planet Uranus. In the later Aquarian Age the creative will of man will have such scope as the world has not dreamed of. It will be set free from the limitations which have held it. When all men are assured of a means of livelihood, how free they will be in *mind*! The freedom of the past in a free country like America is nothing like the freedom which the new age will usher in.

When education is really universal, the moral as well as the mental will be trained, and new ideas will have room to develop in the developing brain. Be not afraid, O world! Three years ago, even we who see far out here had grave doubts for the future of your planet. But the great Masters always told us that the world would pass through its period of trial, still poised on its old axis, and that the *forces which make for order would triumph over the forces which make for disorder*. Have you not noticed in the psychic world a lessening of strain? Have you not noticed an absence of the hostile and adverse beings that in the early months of the war seemed to threaten the earth and you and all men with a triumphant malice? That is a straw which shows the way of "the winds that blow between the worlds."

I am glad that you are a keen observer of psychic states. That faculty of observation will be of use to you in the years that are to come. Those who cannot adjust to new conditions will pass out for a time and return later with the fresh outlook of children, to take up their experience in the new age. There will be much rebellion in the beginning. Things are not so stable as they *seemed* four years ago. The war has proved that they were not really stable. The wave of psychic research that is now sweeping across the world will wear thin the veil between the visible and the invisible. More and more men and women will live in two worlds at the same time; for the two worlds occupy the same space, and their differences are differences of consciousness, of vibration, the latter including a difference in states of matter.

Men will grow more magnetic under the influences that will play upon them. They will affect each other more and more, and that is one reason why greater freedom will be necessary. With the greater sensitiveness which the new time will bring, it will be more difficult for large families to live together a common life. While the tendency is for all mankind to be one family in sympathy, more and more it will be recognized that each man requires privacy for his best development. The tyranny of the family will give place to freedom *in* the family. Strip family life of its tyranny and it may be very charming.

The sensitive and highly charged beings of the new age would explode if they should be obliged to sit every evening round the family "center table," listening to the maunderings of the least progressive among them, who by reason of greater age assumed the right to lay down the law. This does not mean that children will not honor their parents; but under the new dispensation parents will honor their children's need for the individual life, and will give it to them—thereby securing their own freedom. The freedom of the later Aquarian Age will be manifest in the mind. "Heresy" will cease to exist; the word will become obsolete.

The sin against the Holy Ghost will be understood as the attempt to enchain the will of another. Great friendliness will result from this mutual tolerance. We hate only those whom we fear, and in a tolerant world there will be few seeds of hatred. All men will study; the school is only the first stage of study. When man becomes his own schoolmaster he makes great strides. What you know of art, music and literature can give you but a vague idea of what these arts will become in the age that is to follow. Take the catchwords of the immediate past, impressionism, for example. It will be applied to all the arts. Science is only in its swaddling clothes. Aquarius is a sign of air, the old books tell us, and the air holds many secrets which you must take for your own, not only secrets of transportation but psychological secrets. The airplane and psychical research grew up together.

You have not taken the last redoubt of electricity. That also has treasures for you. When you can draw *that* from the air where it hides from you and laughs, you will have little need of coal, and the miners can leave the bowels of the earth and play in the sunshine of the heights. Inventions! I see in the "pattern world" I told you about in my first book many things that would puzzle you down here. New fabrics will be worn before many years, and the patient silkworm will not be the aristocrat it now is.

The human ego is coming into its own. When it loses selfishness it will find itself. That is not a paradox for its own sake, but the statement of a psychological fact.

The seeming chaos will take form, and in it you will find new beauties. I will not conceal from you the knowledge that many will use the word chaos during the reconstruction period. But be at peace. The formless shall take on form. The clairvoyance that is developing in man will help him to see, where the eyes of his old faith would have been blind. He will trust the future and trust his brother, and will not be deceived. The intuition of the soul will point man to the substance which he needs for his wellbeing. Behind and within the air is the ether, which is substance, which is God. And man will take it for his uses, with the consent of God, who joys in giving Himself to His children.

As I said before, the Masters urge the world along in the direction of its destiny; but they are too wise to hurry it. They see the face of the cosmic clock, and they wake the world at the hour of the new sunrise. We are blest in being their servants.

The Watchers

February 3, 1918

I STOOD ONE DAY before a great soul that had renounced the rest in heaven, and questioned him as to the work that called us loudest. What do you think he said? *"Labor with those who fear for the future."* "Are there so many, then, who look forward with apprehension?" I asked. "All those who think and see and have responsibilities are apprehensive," he replied. Then I wandered here and there about America, looking in upon all sorts of men and a few women. And I read in their minds a great uncertainty.

"Sufficient unto the day is the evil thereof," I thought so intensely *at* them that many responded with a hopeful smile. Yes, I can win response from many people when I think strongly enough in their company. The faith of one great soul out here has helped many to stand steady when the winds blew strong against them. He knows that America cannot fail of her destiny; but that she may not take a wrong tack, he would guide the hand and brush the mists from before the eye of the skipper.

There are often mists before the path of the "ship of State" in these gray days. When Wilson took over the railroads, what courage was there! When all is over there will be many to criticize and blame him; but criticism and blame are ever the rewards of those who depersonalize themselves and labor for the good of their country or the world. The man who is great enough to cast his personality overboard is not hurt by criticism. It is only the personality that can be hurt. The soul stands serene and pure above the adverse storms.

I do not advise all men to disregard their personality. Only those who bear great responsibilities may safely become impersonal. The small man, the undeveloped man, could not persuade his soul to take the place of his lesser self. For the soul must be persuaded to descend and dwell in the personality. Most souls are only partially incarnated. The higher self of most men dwells above and apart. It is their Silent Watcher; but it seldom acts save to warn and save. It leaves the lesser self to acquire experience and learn its lessons through suffering and joy, through success and failure. But when the man has so far evolved that his acts become of more than personal significance, then the soul may descend and truly guide and influence the man, for the designs of the soul are ever beyond the personal. It is a conscious part of the great whole, a conscious part of God whom it worships and serves, however the lower self may be immersed in trivialities and blasphemies.

In any man who has not lost his soul the Higher Watcher has an interest. For the Watcher is One and he is many. He is your link with God, Oh, men! He is your link with immortality. You do not meet him merely by dying, for you may dwell long in the astral and lower mental world before meeting him face to face. But if you can ascend after death to the higher regions, you will find him there waiting for you. You may bring to him all the fine fruits of your recent life, and he will enjoy them with you. I have met my soul face to face; but I am unable to remain in the higher regions in peaceful contemplation of his beauty while there is so much work to be done for the races on earth as calls to me now. Bye and bye I shall reascend; but when I go to heaven for a long sojourn you will hear from me no more.

Yes, I too have seen your soul. But I need not describe its face to you, who see it better than I. Cling to it. The failure of mortal friendship has no power to shatter the faith of one who can reach to his own Silent Watcher. And the soul of the faithless friend is pure as his own, and understands all things. Friendships, like loves, are made in heaven, and true friendship cannot die. Its roots are deep in waters of eternity. It is deathless as the Ygdrasil, and its roots are also above and its branches below.

But it is better to fail in business than to fail in friendship. If a man is great and strong enough, he may draw down his soul to dwell with him wherever he may be. Then the man is a whole man, he is an adept. Lincoln is such a man, such a soul. He has become one with his Higher Watcher, and the two that are one can work even in the regions of the astral. But such a marriage of heaven and earth is uncommon, as adepts are uncommon. Your father in heaven is one with the Father, and if you are really one with your father in heaven he can dwell with you even on earth.

The higher souls of men are closer to men now than they have been for ages. The doors have been opened. Grief and terror and pain and devotion to ideals of duty have raised the race of men in three and a half years as it could not have been raised in a hundred years of peace. If the race falls back now, it will be a lost opportunity. But the race will not fall back.

LETTER 28

A Ritual of Fellowship

February 8, 1918

I HAVE BEEN WAITING for you half an hour, as you sat sewing a seam and thinking of your friends in France. It warms the heart now to think of France. The tie between the two great republics is being drawn closer and closer. Shall I tell you an occult secret? The French mixed their blood with ours long ago, and we have loved them ever since. We are now mixing our blood with the blood of France, and France will love us in the days that are to come. It is a ritual of fellowship, that mixing of blood. English and French and Americans and Italians, Irish, Scotch, and all the others. Is there not a foundation for brotherhood? The blended blood cries from the ground for love.

I see in the eyes of the French their feeling for our men as they march by, or help in the little ways to which American boys are accustomed. Never again will they look upon us as queer people from beyond the sea. We have traveled in their country and spent our money and swaggered and talked through our noses; but now we are living and dying with them, and we are brothers of mixed blood. Yes, go back to France when you can. They always loved you because you loved them, but now you will see that they also love your native land.

Recruiting Agents

February 1918

F OR A DAY OR TWO after America declared that a state of war existed, I spent most of my time in going about this country, studying conditions in both worlds. Even before that survey I had a general idea of how matters stood in those worlds; but I wanted to freshen my memory, for I had a great idea. Many times during my life on earth I had told myself that I had a great idea, and sometimes I put it into execution, and sometimes I failed in doing so. But this time I was determined there should be no failure.

When I had seen from my survey that the materials were all at hand, I sought out a great man, spirit, or whatever you choose to call him. Then together we mapped out our campaign. Here are the main points of it: Conservation—where the negative forces should be applied. Construction—with our positive forces. Coordination—with the synthetic forces. We marshaled a group of those strong-minded, strong-willed men and women who had been out here long enough to know not only their way about, but how to impress their thoughts upon material-bodied men and women. These were dispatched here and there, to think, think, think, in the neighborhood of senators and congressmen, chiefs of industry and members of the general public. The burden of their impressed thought was conservation of food, conservation of expenditure, conservation of all material that would be needed for the activities of the war.

Others who were filled with a great love for the land of their latest birth, America, went about in bands instilling their patriotic enthusiasm into the hearts and minds of those millions who had too long taken America as a matter of course. They sang patriotic songs, and though they could not be heard by the ears of earth, the spirit of their singing could be felt, and they accomplished much. Then others, the wisest among old leaders of men, were busy in quelling disorder, in suppressing discontent with the war. Whenever a group of wild-eyed, peace-prating "idealists" got together to talk twaddle, there was one or more of these unseen auditors to put the brakes on responsive enthusiasm to the dangerous principles enunciated.

I will not bore you by giving all the details of this plan of help which we labored to make effective. But there were enrolled more than one million beings out here who have pledged themselves to serve until their services are no longer required. That may not seem to you a great number to help invisibly a nation of more than one hundred millions; but one to every hundred is enough among the active workers, for each is free to choose assistants among those younger in earth experience. To the one who acted as our commander-in-chief, the generals of this auxiliary army made reports, and many were the strange orders he gave them. But no one questioned his wisdom, and the results have proved it over and over.

One time when I wanted to go North, he sent me to the South, and in Mobile I learned why my course was changed. It is a wonder that the legislators at the various capitols have not "seen ghosts" during the last months. Perhaps they have. But men are becoming accustomed to the idea of us now. That is one of the good results of the war. In looking across the border for their loved ones, they may encounter the Teachers, even the angels of their loved ones, and be enlarged in mind. I had an amusing experience in the city of –. There is a "pacifist" there who has a considerable influence among the members of a certain set, and I found that when he began one of his "philosophic" talks to one or more persons, for he has not lectured publicly, I could bewilder him by speaking in his ear and answering his questions in a way that made him wonder. For, strange to say perhaps, he could hear me. But not believing in the possibility of communication between the worlds, he thought he was having "clair-audient hallucinations," and consulted a doctor who told him that he had been brooding too much about the war. The doctor, who was not a pacifist, advised our friend to take up ornithology.

Yes, he is young—and will be young for many incarnations. We have also done our share of recruiting. Those who were later called by the draft were merely encouraged; but there were others who needed only the dream we sent, or the thought we whispered, to move them in the right direction; and when a young man's country is at war, the right direction is generally towards the nearest recruiting station.

There was a boy in—who had been reading about France and the fighting in France with a tightening at the heart, a tightening of horror. He feared the draft. He was not a husky fellow. His labors as bookkeeper in a bank had not developed his leg muscles, and he had a capricious digestion. So he told himself that he would be a failure as a soldier. But one time when in sleep he came out into our world, I met him and invited him to take a stroll with me. Do you think I took him to a battlefield? Oh, no! I took him to an exercise ground. You may wonder how I could do that at night; but it chanced that he had fallen asleep in the daytime. And I think I made it easy for him to see down in the world he had temporarily left—to see the exercise ground. It interested him.

And next day the labor over the ledger seemed duller and more monotonous than usual. And he overheard a girl say to a friend at the paying teller's window, that a sallow faced clerk was not her ideal of a man, that she liked the soldier boys. When he went for a walk after banking hours, I went along with him, and drew his attention to some marching soldiers who had a good band. The boy went home and looked at himself in the mirror and found that he was sallow, and he reminded himself that he was a clerk. So he enlisted. You may wonder why I took so much trouble to gather one uninteresting young man into the fold of Uncle Sam's army, when we had so many subordinate workers at that business. But I had known the boy's father twenty years before, and something he had said influenced *me* towards a decision that enlightened my whole after life.

When that boy returns he will no longer be sallow-faced, and he will be a hero—not a clerk. I like to pay my debts.

The Virus of Disruption

February 16, 1918

"FREEDOM WITH SELF-RESTRAINT and social responsibility" would be a good motto for Americans in the years that are before them. The underground and overground propaganda of Bolshevism, Anarchism, etc., inspired and fed by the forces of destruction, can be successfully combated by the spirit of order, of restraint, of responsibility to the body politic. The end of this war will not be the end of confusion. The world soul has been inoculated with the virus of disruption, and it will need the wills of millions working together for a common end to expel the poison and restore the body of humanity to health and security.

America as we know it was born of protest against oppression, and the love of liberty, father and mother, positive and negative, in the old days. If now the protest against oppression degenerates into the protest against all restraint, and if the love of liberty degenerates into the love of licence, then I may tell you that those who cannot govern themselves have to be governed from outside. The human race is passing through a period of initiation. The morally weak and the weak of will are always in danger of being carried away. The spirit of destruction finds them ready tools with which to work its will.

The kingdom of heaven is not immediately at hand,

and full seven years will be needed to *settle the consciousness* of mankind after the shaking-up it has received. The dregs, as usual in such cases, have risen and diffused themselves throughout the fluid of the cup. If there were only a dozen people in the United States who understood or could be made to understand the *occult forces* behind the present universal unrest, and if these twelve could work together with unity of purpose, some here, some there, with the pen, the voice and the will, under a leader, those twelve might lead the people out of the wilderness. But where are they? Every leader knows that in unity is strength. And I may mention the opposite law, that in disunity is disintegration.

Bolshevist and anarchist! Finding the world not to their liking, and being unable to adjust to environment so as to satisfy their love of power, or their love of ease, these people have devoted themselves to destroying the society in which they are unsuccessful. They believe themselves right. There is so much of the divine in almost the worst man, that he has to believe he is working for the right even when he is working for evil. It is necessary for a murderer to justify his act in order to do it, unless he is swept away by blind passion, and then he seeks to justify passion itself. The heart of man is superior to the brain of man. Almost anyone can feel a good impulse; but the man who can think independently of his passions is rare and isolate. Popular education does not mean universal reasoning power. But popular education is the beginning; it is the seed out of which will grow the tree of world-intellect.

I have told you of the reign of love that is at length to comfort the hearts of mankind; but I have not told you that it is coming tomorrow or the next day. If you can get away from the personal and the temporary, and see life and the movements of cycles in perspective, you will see how temporary unrest is only a stage by the way. He who adjusts to environment adjusts even to unrest. Remember that. The supple tree feels the wind, but its roots cling tight to the soil and the rock of individuality. Be like the supple tree, America. In the wind that sweeps across the world, cling tight to the soil of freedom and the rock of *social responsibility*. You can save the world if you do not lose your hold on the soil and the rock that have steadied and sustained you.

The anxious eyes of a Europe in conflagration are turned in your direction, your friends with hope, your enemies with dread. When you threw the weight of your strong young body into the scales of justice, you changed the destiny of the world. Yes, it was your destiny to do it. All you who have studied "occultism," which merely means knowledge too profound to be understood by the material-minded—you who have studied occultism know that to the candidate for initiation come trials and tests, and that without them he cannot go on. Think of the human race as a candidate for initiation. If your mind is developed beyond the minds of your fellows— you, and you, and you—do not forget that you are united to them by an indissoluble bond. You cannot break away from the race. You may rise above it as the Master does, or sink beneath it as the lost souls do; but the link between you and those other fragments of God can only be broken at your peril.

The Master works for the race, knowing well that he cannot safely ignore it. Even if he made himself equal with the gods and desired to build a world of his own, he would have to take the substance for it from the common reservoir of substance. If like a spider he could spin his world-web for himself, he would have to eat the common substance to sustain himself in his power. You may as well love the race, for you cannot escape it altogether. Even if you rise and dwell in the thin air of the kingdom of the mind, you will feel the wind currents from your fellows above and below. Some will deny this, but I have made the test.

I recently sought a high place for rest. But the needs of the world pulled me back. The greatest need of the world for the next few years will be the knowledge of the law of conservation. Retain, O world! The treasures you have labored for throughout the centuries, and discard only the worn-out garments and utensils. The wooden plough and the wooden shoe are no longer needed in a wisely ordered world; but the sciences and the arts you will need, and the Gothic cathedrals you destroy can never be replaced.

LETTER 31

The Altar Fire

February 18, 1918

LWAYS THE PULL OF the opposites! In all the talk of internationalism, let us not forget nationalism. The enemy of the present hour made great use of it, but he did not reckon with its opposite. It is not true internationalism to support spies as commercial agents in all the countries of earth. America of all nations is best fitted to carry on her standards: Each for all, and all for each. But in her love for other races, for other nationalities, let her not forget to strengthen and uphold her own.

"My country, 'tis of Thee!" As that sentiment grows ever stronger in your heart, so will your justice to other nations make you recognize that their countries are of them. For your country was not built upon the idea of world domination, but of freedom—for yourselves and for all men. Your president has been called a maker of phrases. That is good. A man who can make phrases that shall carry themselves around the world can influence the thought of the world. "To make the world safe for democracy." Those words will go down the centuries.

You Americans who love the storied lands of Europe, do not underestimate this land that gave you birth. It is great as the greatest now, and its clock has not yet struck twelve noon. It is still morning in America. The present day American is the ancestor of the man of the Sixth

Race. From many stocks he will spring, and his blood will be blended from that of all the races which have preceded him. He will be unique in his qualities. No man of the older races can imitate him, for his consciousness will be his own. A man is not, as you have so often said, of flesh and blood and bone and sinew, but a man is a state of consciousness. It is because you recognize their state of consciousness as being themselves, that men and women reveal themselves to you. If—or when—you go back to Europe to live, do not forget your country. Do not remain too long away from it, lest you lose touch with that unique consciousness which shall flower in the Sixth Race.

Yes, a great art will grow up in America. After another fifty years it will be ripe. Let us hope it will not begin to rot thereafter, but like a sound American apple preserve its solidity for a long time. This war is good for America. It is not well for a race to have so great a material success without some pain and struggle. It is pain that mellows the heart. America has not yet found her soul, but she will find it. Those Americans who are now broken-hearted are finding their souls. France found her soul a long time ago, and she is now finding her divinity. Would she have found it but for suffering? The Christ upon the cross is greater than the Christ at the marriage supper in Cana of Galilee.

If I had not wanted you to write this book, I should have sent you back to London, that you might experience the strain of air raids and insufficient food. I should have sent you back to France, that you might see and touch and minister to the wounded. Though you have endured the strain of the astral world at war, you have not yet

seen and touched and tasted the agony of physical suffering that the women of France have seen and touched
and tasted. But you cannot live and suffer in too many
worlds at once. Do you not think that our American boys
who are fighting now in France will be greater for the experience—whether they live or die? Life in material form
is not the only life, and those who make the great sacrifice will gain more than they lose. It is sublime to die for
an ideal. "To make the world safe for democracy."

America is better known to Europeans now than she
has been before. Many of you will go and come, as you
have done in the past; and a few of you will vitalize the
mutual understanding between America and Europe.
But you can do that only by glorifying your own nation-
ality in your hearts. I do not mean flaunting it. Let it
burn as an altar fire, in the secret temple of your being.

Also available from
White Crow Books

Marcus Aurelius—*The Meditations*
ISBN 978-1-907355-20-2

Elsa Barker—*Letters from a Living Dead Man*
ISBN 978-1-907355-83-7

Elsa Barker—*War Letters from the Living Dead Man*
ISBN 978-1-907355-85-1

Elsa Barker—*Last Letters from the Living Dead Man*
ISBN 978-1-907355-87-5

Richard Maurice Bucke—*Cosmic Consciousness*
ISBN 978-1-907355-10-3

G. K. Chesterton—*The Everlasting Man*
ISBN 978-1-907355-03-5

G. K. Chesterton—*Heretics*
ISBN 978-1-907355-02-8

G. K. Chesterton—*Orthodoxy*
ISBN 978-1-907355-01-1

Arthur Conan Doyle—*The Edge of the Unknown*
ISBN 978-1-907355-14-1

Arthur Conan Doyle—*The New Revelation*
ISBN 978-1-907355-12-7

Arthur Conan Doyle—*The Vital Message*
ISBN 978-1-907355-13-4

Arthur Conan Doyle with Simon Parke—*Conversations with Arthur Conan Doyle*
ISBN 978-1-907355-80-6

Leon Denis with Arthur Conan Doyle—*The Mystery of Joan of Arc*
ISBN 978-1-907355-17-2

The Earl of Dunraven—*Experiences in Spiritualism with D. D. Home*
ISBN 978-1-907355-93-6

Meister Eckhart with Simon Parke—*Conversations with Meister Eckhart*
ISBN 978-1-907355-18-9

Kahlil Gibran—*The Forerunner*
ISBN 978-1-907355-06-6

Kahlil Gibran—*The Madman*
ISBN 978-1-907355-05-9

Kahlil Gibran—*The Prophet*
ISBN 978-1-907355-04-2

Kahlil Gibran—*Sand and Foam*
ISBN 978-1-907355-07-3

Kahlil Gibran—*Jesus the Son of Man*
ISBN 978-1-907355-08-0

Kahlil Gibran—*Spiritual World*
ISBN 978-1-907355-09-7

Hermann Hesse—*Siddhartha*
ISBN 978-1-907355-31-8

D. D. Home—*Incidents in my Life Part 1*
ISBN 978-1-907355-15-8

Mme. Dunglas Home; edited, with an Introduction, by Sir Arthur Conan Doyle—*D. D. Home: His Life and Mission*
ISBN 978-1-907355-16-5

Andrew Lang—*The Book of Dreams and Ghosts*
ISBN 978-1-907355-97-4

Edward C. Randall—*Frontiers of the Afterlife*
ISBN 978-1-907355-30-1

Lucius Annaeus Seneca—*On Benefits*
ISBN 978-1-907355-19-6

Rebecca Ruter Springer—*Intra Muros—My Dream of Heaven*
ISBN 978-1-907355-11-0

W. T. Stead—*After Death or Letters from Julia: A Personal Narrative*
ISBN 978-1-907355-89-9

Leo Tolstoy, edited by Simon Parke—*Tolstoy's Forbidden Words*
ISBN 978-1-907355-00-4

Leo Tolstoy—*A Confession*
ISBN 978-1-907355-24-0

Leo Tolstoy—*The Gospel in Brief*
ISBN 978-1-907355-22-6

Leo Tolstoy—*The Kingdom of God is Within You*
ISBN 978-1-907355-27-1

Leo Tolstoy—*My Religion—What I Believe*
ISBN 978-1-907355-23-3

Leo Tolstoy—*On Life*
ISBN 978-1-907355-91-2

Leo Tolstoy—*23 Tales*
ISBN 978-1-907355-29-5

Leo Tolstoy—*What is Religion and other writings*
ISBN 978-1-907355-28-8

Leo Tolstoy—*Work While Ye Have the Light*
ISBN 978-1-907355-26-4

Leo Tolstoy with Simon Parke—*Conversations with Tolstoy*
ISBN 978-1-907355-25-7

Howard Williams with an Introduction by Leo Tolstoy—*The Ethics of Diet: An Anthology of Vegetarian Thought*
ISBN 978-1-907355-21-9

All titles available as eBooks, and select titles available in Audiobook format from www.whitecrowbooks.com

49 - Falsehoods
50 - "Fighting"

LaVergne, TN USA
12 December 2010
208454LV00001B/102/P